TAU LEWIS

VOX POPULI, VOX DEI

CLARION

TAU LEWIS

V

Contents

Curator's Note: The Ghost
Ebony L. Haynes

One of Tau Lewis's greatest musical influences is the Jamaican roots-reggae singer Winston Rodney. Rodney's signature ghostly chants, dubbed-out psychedelic repetition, and sad yet hopeful vocal work make up the heavy roots sound that is encompassed by his stage name, Burning Spear. His polythematic oeuvre deals with Pan-Africanism, doctrinal systems, and Jamaican political discourse. His 1975 album *Marcus Garvey* weaves these themes together to create a potent message of faith and political radicalism, making him a hero in Jamaica and cementing his legacy within the heavy roots philosophy and movement. Rodney's music oscillates around the title of Lewis's exhibition at 52 Walker, *Vox Populi, Vox Dei* (Latin for "the voice of the people [is] the voice of God"). For Lewis, the phrase becomes a descriptor of our relationship to our own belief systems, calling into question the source of authenticity and truth.

At 52 Walker, Lewis's monumental masks—the latest works in her continuing exploration of anthropomorphic forms informed by those in Yoruban mask dramas—draw inspiration from the work of the Nigerian playwright Wole Soyinka, as well as from classical Greek and Roman mythology and drama. Tiana Reid's text in this volume illuminates these pathways and examines the link between theater and the eighteenth-century tract that gives the show its title. The gallery's polygonal shape situated the viewer centrally on stage, surrounded by Lewis's congregation of forms, which seemed to be engaged in an inaudible conversation across the space. Visitors activated the drama at play by their presence. Figures from the same body of work installed in viewing rooms downstairs served as counterparts to the characters above, embodying different aspects of the same being. Lewis's practice is iterative—her bodies of work are populated by many of the same characters or spirits in various guises.

This work incorporates material drawn from an archive of her own clothing, donations from family and friends, a trove of abandoned coats from a Long Island furrier, and recycled items obtained from FABSCRAP. Together, these strips and swaths of fabric, layered and sewn, and carried from one work to the next, echo the genetic thread, or the "material DNA," that links Lewis's beings in a genealogical tree. As the material source archives have become more anonymous, chance encounters with someone's name written on a tag, another's embroidered initials on a shirt cuff, unique labels, and even others' smells held within the fabric have become significant in a larger act of world-building that Lewis achieves with her characters. The sculptures take on a spiritual or mythological presence through their blending of personal and collective histories and memories. Lewis's process also allows her entities, and the characters they share, to be reimagined from work to work, a nested approach to upcycling that develops the narrative thread of occupying both grounded and heavenly realms. This show is the work of angels.

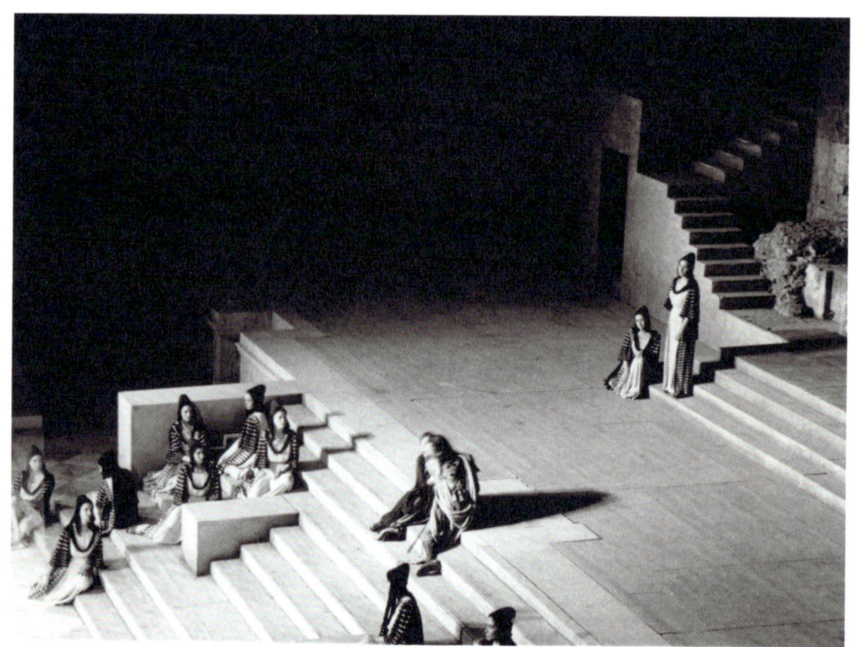

Staged production of Euripides's *Phoenissae*, n.d.

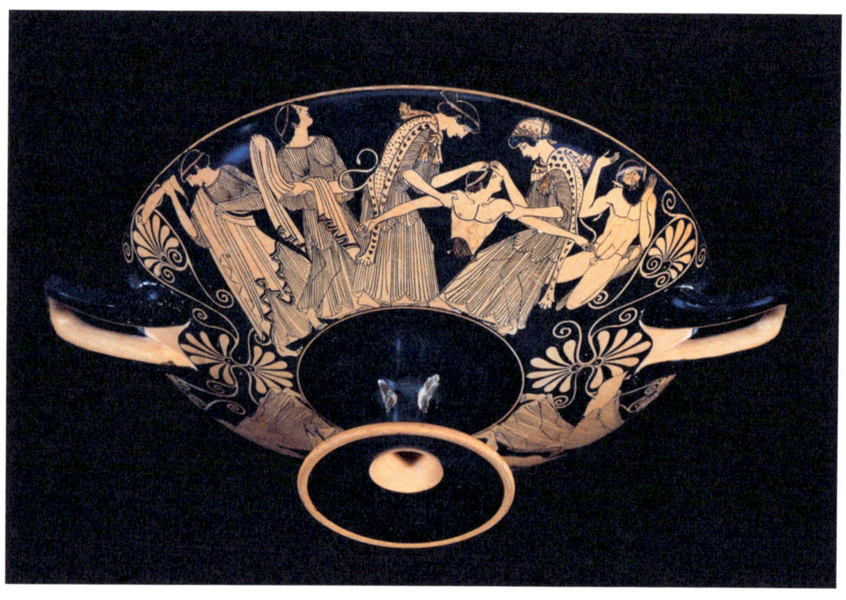

Douris, Red-Figure Cup Showing the Death of Pentheus (exterior)
and a Maenad (interior), c. 480 BC
Terracotta

9

What the People Are Like:
Voices from Without
Tiana Reid

PENTHEUS: I shall have order! Let the city
  know at once
Pentheus is here to give back order and sanity.
To think those reports which came to be
  abroad are true!
Not padded or strained. Disgustingly true
  in detail.
If anything reality beggars the report. It's
  disgusting!
I leave the country, I'm away only a moment
Campaigning to secure our national frontiers.
  And what happens?
Behind me—chaos! The city in uproar. Well,
  let everyone
Know I've returned to re-impose order. Order!
And tell it to the women especially, those
Promiscuous bearers of this new disease.
—Wole Soyinka, *The Bacchae of Euripides:*
A Communion Rite (1973)[1]

Listening to those voices raging in the dark,
Selina often thought of the family who had lived
there before them.
—Paule Marshall, *Brown Girl, Brownstones* (1959)[2]

A silent slave is not liked by masters or overseers. "Make a noise," "make a noise," and "bear
a hand," are the words usually addressed to the
slaves when there is silence amongst them. This
may account for the almost constant singing
heard in the southern states. There was, gener-
ally, more or less singing among the teamsters,
as it was one means of letting the overseer
know where they were, and that they were moving on with the work.
—Frederick Douglass, *My Bondage and My*
Freedom (1855)[3]

Imagine a group of actors onstage in the 1970s,
rehearsing a play. They are at the historic Old Vic
Theatre in London. The director is working from
a text wherein the prefatory production note
reads, in part: "The Slaves and the Bacchantes
should be as mixed a cast as is possible, testifying
to their varied origins. Solely because of the 'hol-
lering' style suggested for the Slave Leader's solo
in the play, it is recommended that this character
be fully negroid."[4]

It is not difficult to fantasize about what it could
all mean: drama as constitutive of empire, the late
twentieth-century stage as a multicultural inheri-
tance, the libidinal illusion of racial purity. But what
I really mean for us to do is to picture a rehearsal
for the Nigerian writer Wole Soyinka's *The Bacchae
of Euripides: A Communion Rite*, an adaptation of
Euripides's tragedy *Bacchae* that he wrote in exile in
Britain and which opened at the Old Vic Theatre in
the summer of 1973.

The interpretations of the subtitle, *A Communion
Rite*, abound: postcolonial rewritings, eucharistic
tropes, the salted wounds of canonical world literature, the politics of racial casting, the ferment
of political theology, the sustaining intoxication
of spirituality. "*The Bacchae*," Soyinka writes in his
introduction, "belongs to that sparse body of plays
which evoke awareness of a particular moment in
a people's history, yet imbue that moment with a
hovering, eternal presence."[5] Soyinka himself did
more than evoke awareness, instead remaking the
Greek classic as a rite, a clamorous feast, a cultish
mania. His authorial hand was strong, with stage
directions oriented toward frenzy, speech, and
movement. In the production note he states clearly,
"Any cuts in the text, dictated by production neces-
sities must NOT be permitted to affect the essential dimension of a Nature feast."

At 52 Walker, Tau Lewis's exhibition *Vox Populi,
Vox Dei* stages conversations with literature that
are especially inflected by theater and performance. One of Lewis's jumping-off points for
this body of work is Soyinka's *The Bacchae of
Euripides*, which is based on the Greek myth of
King Pentheus of Thebes and his mother, who
are punished by his cousin Dionysus for not
worshiping him.[6] The circularity of influence,

its ability to flow even as so-called originals are turned around, reworked, reused, and abused, is part of the breakthrough of imagination.

As evidenced by the extensive research bibliography accompanying *Vox Populi, Vox Dei*, Lewis also draws on literatures that emphasize transformation and transgression, such as the feminist anarcho-futurisms of Ursula K. Le Guin and the black queer sci-fi eroticisms of Samuel R. Delany. But her use of theater as a reference point, combined with the invocation of an eighteenth-century British Whig party tract, reveals a sustaining interest in her practice: the idea that democracy relies on theater in its simultaneous making and dispossessing of the people. The early eighteenth-century British Empire was not near the violent height it would reach when the tract was published, but *The Judgment of Whole Kingdoms and Nations, Concerning the Rights, Power, and Prerogative of Kings, and the Rights, Privileges, and Properties of the People* is considered a textual authority of Western democracy and its accompanying fetishizations. Variously attributed to Lord Somers, Daniel Defoe, John Dunton, and Gilbert Burnet, it leans on the idea of the voice and the idea of the people as requirements for liberal democracy. The voice of the people—what a basic yet petulant pronouncement, fueling ideologies across the political spectrum.

Vox populi: The vocality of the people cannot be guaranteed. Nor can the existence of the people themselves. According to *The Judgment of Whole Kingdoms and Nations*, which was first published under the title *Vox Populi, Vox Dei: Being True Maxims of Government*, in 1709:

> To resist any of these Powers in the Administration or executing of the Laws is a Sin, and every Sin in its Nature is damnable, without Repentance and Forgiveness of God: Yet these Powers may be resisted, prosecuted, and punished, according to the Nature of his, or their Crimes. Now, can any Man say, that these Magistrates are ordained of God, or have their Power from God, any more than that all Men are ordained of God, and have their Lives and Strength from him, which is their Power, and in the executing of this Power, they have Power to do Good or Evil? Before they are chosen Magistrates, they have no more Power than other Men, but when chosen, the Law is their Power, beyond which they cannot go without incurring the Penalty thereof.[7]

To this end, tyrannical legal structures inculcate a sense of spiritual power. Not necessarily always on the flip side of this sensibility, black political agency also functions with recourse to a certain vocal precondition while also correcting the illusions of a fixable, singular, and general voice.

Black cultural production is more than a call for multiples—many or more voices, many or more people. Proponents of democracy cite its Greek origins: the rule (*kratos*) of the people (*demos*). Black critical practice attends to the limits of inherited theory. Some left-leaning liberals argue that we have not achieved "true" democracy, that there is more to fight for. Others suggest that we have reached the apotheosis of democracy: that exclusion, dispossession, demoralization, and exploitation are in fact the rule, not the exception.

In the essay "Afrarealism and the Black Matrix: Maroon Philosophy at Democracy's Border," Joy James writes, "Afrarealism recognizes two coterminous phenomena: democracy as a boundary defining freedom through captivity, and maroon philosophy at the borders reimagining freedom through flight. Afrarealism does not equate democracy with freedom as some black philosophy does. Rather, Afrarealism's journey moves adjacent to a democracy originating and reproducing amid racial captivity and racial rape."[8] Maroon philosophy is a radical or radicalized black theory. It is a politics that focuses on reproductive labor in the face of intimate state violence.

In her conclusion, with the subhead "Grieving Beauty," James cites Euripides's *Medea*, writing:

> In Euripides's play *Medea*, the Greek chorus of slave women plead against and beautifully grieve Medea's sovereign vengeance expressed in the murder of her and Jason's children and his child-bride. Lacking grieving beauty as an impetus to act, the chorus does not flee or impede the slave mistress's homicidal terror. Euripides, as author, refuses the slaves the agency of defiance,

the dance in resistance. They lack the wisdom that rebellion inevitably follows violent tyranny. Hence these women lack the beauty of survival, they have no concept of *maroonage*.[9]

James's critique of democracy concludes with an acknowledgment of its constitutive edges: those borders that both contain and exceed the terms of democracy. Lewis, too, is pointing to democracy in order to point outside it. Lewis's anthemic sculptures stage a range of resistive refuges, what James calls the "beauty of survival" in the edges of history.

To what extent is the voice of the people an impossible abstraction? Voice in Soyinka's *The Burden of Memory*, like in his *Bacchae of Euripides*, like in Lewis's *Vox Populi, Vox Dei*, lives among godliness.[10] I could call voice god, I could call it spirit, I could call it anything other than my body, but the simple point I am making is that it is called, it is imagined. I don't remember when I first encountered Lewis's clamorous work, but it got under my skin, and it hasn't left since. Lewis follows in a fertile creative tradition of black artists, forging sculptural assemblages out of textiles, shells, and other found materials, and producing narratives that suffuse history with presence.[11]

At the heart of Lewis's practice is truly practice, over and over again. With its elucidation of the patchwork-like quality of singular forms, fragmentation, and repetition, Lewis's work helps to uncover openings in what Susan Stewart has called, drawing on Max Horkheimer and Theodor Adorno, the "illusion of individuation."[12] Each of Lewis's characters comprises manifold parts, so that any prefiguration of persona is too tangled to cohere. I see, too, an almost addictive need to collect, layer, and tangle, like Hubert Harrison's, like Betye Saar's.[13]

Vox populi, vox Dei: "The voice of the people [is] the voice of God" is how the Latin is typically translated. The singularity of voice becomes multiple, and through its multiplication it becomes the ultimate voice, a divine voice. In *Vox Populi, Vox Dei*, six oversize masklike sculptures are arranged on faceted walls, simulating the form of a gathering. Each work is striking as a whole, overwhelming almost, but the details push each

quite further, more outside of itself, as with the open nylon threads and repurposed leather scraps in *Mater Dei* (2022; p. 39).

A peopled voice underlies much of Lewis's approach to art making, but the Western historical idea of "people" isn't quite right, either. Lewis's sculptures, evocative of plant and animal life, bear perhaps some resemblance to human shapes but clearly aren't people at all, making them, in a certain sense, monsters. Here, voice is a form aspiring toward aesthetic communication. Voice starts with a self but cannot end there, as it dreams for intelligibility with others. Sometimes the other is God, an unguaranteed communion, a flicker of flight.

Within the gallery, and partly due to the size of Lewis's sculptures, there is a feeling of monumentality, reminiscent of an ancient theater, this sense that we are among ruins. The sensorium built by movement through the space is anchored by the walls, which form a polygonal shape. The viewer steps into something, something grand, a stage and a cavern filled with ends and beginnings all messed up. With sharp corners, the gallery is not a circle, not a sister circle, not a prayer circle. The exhibition's title suggests a Roman amphitheater, an underworld democracy, an ethical-aesthetic experience. In his introduction to *The Bacchae of Euripides*, Soyinka writes that "the ritual, sublimated or expressive, is both social therapy and reaffirmation of group solidarity, a hankering back to the origins and formation of guilds and phratries."[14] The viewer is somewhere in-between, drawn away from linear time into Lewis's multiversed studies.

What if the anthropomorphic sculptures—inspired by Yoruban mask dramas—aren't the actors but instead the audience? Extending the concerns of Lewis's earlier work through her new dramas, *Vox Populi, Vox Dei* can be read as bearing the impossibility of the "populi," a word in translation and mired in Western intellectual traditions and its disenchantments. Lewis does not suggest a redress of democracy's violences. By unpacking and then reconstructing "the voice" of "the people," she introduces us to a level of critical spirituality that is meant to both rise above and seep below governmentality that takes its shape as an anti-black state.

"Giving voice to the voiceless" is a somewhat banal phrase reminiscent of twentieth-century activist-feminist language of "unsilencing." In black literary history, voice is sometimes a metaphor for the unsilencing of the oppressed while it also presents communication as beauty, survival as a necessary aesthetic for political creativity. Black print culture especially held a commitment to voice as a political strategy. For instance, in the first issue of the monthly black left newspaper *Freedom*, which was published from 1950 to 1955, Paul Robeson outlined the goals of the newspaper in his opening editorial: "FREEDOM will be a voice for the poor and disinherited among us. Its pages are dedicated to the needs of the sharecropper, the wage-earner, the housewife; the student and youth searching the future for direction, the mother yearning for peace, the professional proscribed by prejudice, the small businessman crushed by monopoly."[15]

Some of Lewis's materials are recognizable (belt buckles, buttons, shells, thread, textiles, fur, coat linings, leather, beads, paint, stones); others not so much. For example, what is "shagreen," a material listed as part of *Trident* (2022; p. 43)?[16] In *Mater Dei, Resurrector* (2022; p. 25), *Saint Mozelle* (2022; p. 33), *Ivory Gate* (2022; p. 29), and *Trident*, everything flails everywhere. Open stitch, open wound. Insides visible. Guts loose. By contrast, *Homonoia* (2022; p. 47) is cleaner—harmonious, if you consider the etymology of the work's title—held together by more precise shapes and symmetry. Cleaner but not clean—still textured, still with stitching exposed, as if to say, I'm here, the work is here, the labor has been here.

A suggestion for the viewer of any of Lewis's work is to look around, look under, as much as possible. Contort yourself, flex, bend, and jump. Below the deep earthly purples and reds of *Homonoia*, under where the chin might be, there is a heart. And it makes one wonder what details are on top, too high up for the eye to see. These reorientations demand a shifted worldview. One must rearrange oneself to survive.

In these Yoruban-mask-inspired forms, crowns or horns or tentacles splay from the top of the heads. *Homonoia* has a crown made of tentacles that are like eyes. Do the others have eyes? Are their eyes closed or not? *Resurrector* has horns fashioned from gauze. *Ivory Gate* counts among its many materials fossilized teeth, so at least I can say teeth exist. But where are they? What is really showing up are curlicues hanging down, little makeshift cones. Individually, Lewis's sculptures are dazzling, brilliant, beautiful. But they need each other. *Vox Populi, Vox Dei* stretches the trajectory of Lewis's work by concerning itself, materially, with her old scraps, each shred accumulating as if referencing the artist's career overall. Everywhere you stand, the masks are looking at you, acquiring a politics of figurative sculpture. A colossal playfulness so intense it inches toward a madness that oozes from Lewis's cultural forms. Her latest funk-forward personalities (*Trident, Saint Mozelle, Ivory Gate*) overwhelm the atmosphere.

Lewis puts her figures in the room with you. They are there as you are there. What dangles—earrings, scraps, vines—creates shadows on the wall. On Instagram, Lewis further closes the distance, minimizing the physical space between her and her forms, sometimes touching, hugging, and moving them, not quite like a child with a doll but maybe like an inventor manufacturing a superhuman image, or as with *Homonoia* (2022; p. 51), a designer sculpting a supermodel with bulbous shoulders, like a baby quarterback, her hands posed over the mermaid fin. For Lewis, sculpture and assemblage are united by narrative, or what the artist calls "world-building." Each stitch is emblematic of labor, of collecting, sorting, and uniting assorted materials. Guided by Lewis's social performance, a strangeness often lingers in her juicy palette, sometimes giving and taking within the same series, still wrecking at the edge of interpretation.

The embodiment of hopeful refusal and collaborative imagination thrusts outward, over and against ravished individualism. The art world wants to maintain its integrity if only to maintain its money and power, conditioning access to art. But it does not, could not, hold a monopoly on the flourishing of creativity and imagination. But maybe it does monopolize "the discourse" through its usual thefts. ("Iraq Reclaims 17,000 Looted Artifacts, Its Biggest-Ever Repatriation," reads an August 3,

2021, *New York Times* online headline on the return of stolen antiquities held by the Museum of the Bible and Cornell University.) How can the fruit of rebellion not be eaten up by bloated corporatization? How can we erect shields against neutralization and co-optation? How can we prevent institutions' further hypocrisy, neutralized in soggy mission statements? What world could we make instead of the art world? What if art were public property? What if art weren't property at all? What if property didn't exist? What are other avenues for sustaining art—that is to say, life? What do we owe each other?

These are all questions that Lewis poses, questions about the mix of ethics and spirituality as a kind of choreography, the people's full participation in art as something we can only imagine and yet must imagine. I wonder, while observing the spatial tonality of *Vox Populi, Vox Dei*, does this radically embodied imagination consist of the artist's spiritual turn, her ongoing bravura to create something out of things that have been deemed nothings? If prayerful chance reigns in her overarching narrative, it is executed with a surrender and benevolence.

I will begin to end by bringing in a detail of an image of Lewis's *The Octonaut (I can be my own hands to hold)* (2019), installed at Oakville Galleries in the Greater Toronto Area. The figure has outstretched arms, an invitation recalling a line from Keguro Macharia's *Frottage: Frictions of Intimacy across the Black Diaspora*, "I invite you to imagine with me."[17] But in Lewis's hands, the invitation also appears wounded, haunted by world history, indexing an empty space of social isolation and unfulfillable desire. Looking *The Octonaut* in the face—as its parenthetical title declares self-sufficiency, *I can be my own hands to hold*—I find resonances with the laboring worlds I have attempted to trace in this essay: performance, enclosure, democracy, imagination, uncanny countenance, voice.

As M. NourbeSe Philip ends her poetry book *She Tries Her Tongue, Her Silence Softly Breaks* with the "absence of writing," openness and blankness is as good as any way to end this essay.[18] The feeling of having nothing more to say, nothing more to fight for or against in the face of indescribable pasts and

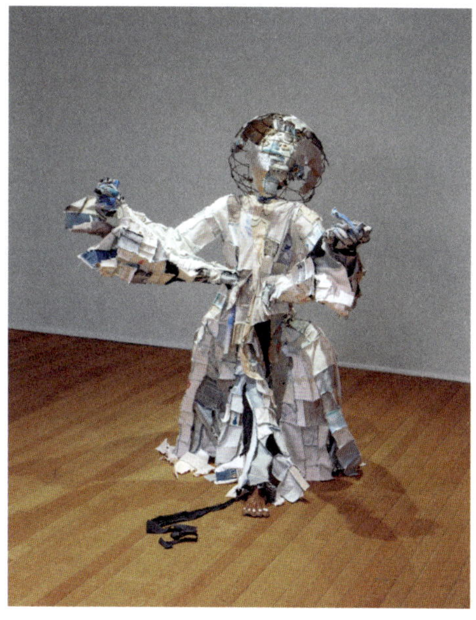

Tau Lewis, *The Octonaut (I can be my own hands to hold)* (2019), installed in *Tau Lewis: Sparkle's Map Home*, Oakville Galleries, Oakville, Ontario, 2020

spectacular presents, is only an untenable affective impasse; an "answerable analytic future" that Katherine McKittrick has warned is "condemned to death"; an "unfinished" urgency similar to Dylan Rodríguez's call for a black studies that "actively occupies (that is, actively and insurgently inhabits) the impasse of anti-black genocide and works within it."[19] Despite the feeling of deadlock, finding comfort in the ambiguity and ambivalence that silence might provide is not enough, and might further reconstitute the trap of language that Philip conveys in *She Tries Her Tongue*.

I end with voice's opposition, silence, as there is something left to be written around Douglass's line that "a silent slave is not liked by masters or overseers." In *My Bondage and My Freedom*, Douglass gets after a certain command for voice, for expressivity, a demand of song that supposedly signals to the slave master a psychic and sonic assurance of productivity. Song here is prefigured or framed not only as spirit or essence but also as a signal of subjection. Thinking about silence in this way troubles categories of agency and resistance and how they come to us as specters, or through what Saidiya

Hartman has broadly called the entanglements of "terror and enjoyment."[20] In Douglass's scene, the enforced refusal of silence is a mechanism of control and containment. In that moment "when there is silence amongst them," Douglass narrates an interruption by a master or an overseer. And what follows: the imperative mood. "Make a noise" is another command to get to work.

Silence's critical function in Douglass's narrative might bring us closer to thinking through its use for something like the ethical or the political ("as opposed to mere politics," in the words of Richard Iton).[21] And yet, as Lewis spins around those opaque claims of the voice of the people as the voice of god, there is also always ambivalence in the work of silence, in the sense that different gestures and relationships to silence can have different meanings and ethical impulses at different times and in different places. In other words, silence, like voice, should not be romanticized for its capacity for a declarative way forward.

Lewis's play between voice, silence, and the divine dislocates a pressure on telos and instead insists on a sometimes muddled and trepidatious orientation, an aesthetics unrecognizable and unimaginable as labor, a work that is always being done without working for certain ("working" as in functioning or operating), a poetics mining any aspiration to close the stage curtains. There is an "incapacity of humankind to create structures of law, principles of morality, or hierarchies of government without a reliance on the imaginary," says Lewis of what Iton calls a "commitment to the practice of disclosure" as a strategy of "confounding options" that rejects "false happy endings."[22] In her sculptures, Lewis recognizes that giving voice is also a practice that takes away.

Notes

1 Wole Soyinka, *The Bacchae of Euripides: A Communion Rite* (New York: W. W. Norton, 1973), p. 27.

2 Paule Marshall, *Brown Girl, Brownstones* (New York: Feminist Press, 1981), p. 51.

3 Frederick Douglass, *My Bondage and My Freedom* (New York: Penguin Classics, 2003), p. 74.

4 Soyinka, *The Bacchae of Euripides*, p. 234.

5 Soyinka, *The Bacchae of Euripides*, p. vi.

6 I can't help but think of the Martinican poet and politician Aimé Césaire's *Une Tempête* here, a paradigmatic example of the anticolonial adaptation of a canonical European text, which then gets anesthetized into the "postcolonial" literature.

7 *The Judgment of Whole Kingdoms and Nations, Concerning the Rights, Power, and Prerogative of Kings, and the Rights, Privileges, and Properties of the People* (London: T. Harrison, 1710), p. 64.

8 Joy James, "Afrarealism and the Black Matrix: Maroon Philosophy at Democracy's Border," *The Black Scholar* 43, no. 4 (Winter 2013), p. 124.

9 James, "Afrarealism and the Black Matrix," p. 128.

10 Soyinka asserts in the introduction to *The Burden of Memory*: "Unlike the theologian, who takes his voice from the realms of deities, the poet appropriates the voice of the people and the full burden of their memory. Where he invokes the gods and the ancestors (as in the case of René Depestre or Birago Diop), it is usually to make them serve the agenda of peoples, to execute their judgment on history and minister to the pangs of their memory." Wole Soyinka, *The Burden of Memory, the Muse of Forgiveness* (New York: Oxford University Press, 1998), p. 21.

11 See also Tiana Reid, "Tau Lewis's 'Secret Objects,'" *Topical Cream* (June 18, 2018), https://topicalcream.org/features/tau-lewiss-secret-objects/; "What You Have, When You Have It: Landscape and the Figural in the Sculptures of Tau Lewis," *Flash Art* (November 2018–January 2019), pp. 50–57; and "Groundations," *Canadian Art* (September 14, 2020), https://canadianart.ca/features/tau-lewis-groundations/.

12 Susan Stewart, *The Open Studio: Essays on Art and Aesthetics* (Chicago: University of Chicago Press, 2005), p. 41.

13 In the 2020 documentary *Betye Saar: Taking Care of Business*, directed by Christine Turner, the American collage and assemblage superstar Betye Saar said, when discussing her work, that she is a "recycler."

14 Soyinka, *The Bacchae of Euripides*, p. xi.

15 Paul Robeson, "A New Voice," *Freedom* (November 1950), p. 4. In his column, Robeson echoes the editorial, stating that he wishes to make *Freedom* "the real voice of the oppressed masses of the Negro people and a true weapon for all progressive Americans." Paul Robeson, "Paul Robeson's Column," *Freedom* (November 1950), p. 4. He also goes beyond the United States, linking the newspaper's reach to the continent of Africa, the Caribbean, Latin America, China, Russia, and the world at large.

16 According to *Merriam-Webster*, a shagreen is "an untanned leather covered with small granulations and usually dyed green; the rough skin of various sharks and rays when covered with small close-set tubercles." *Merriam-Webster Collegiate Dictionary*, 11th ed. (2014), s.v. "shagreen."

17 Keguro Macharia, *Frottage: Frictions of Intimacy across the Black Diaspora* (New York: New York University Press, 2019), p. 30.

18 M. NourbeSe Philip, "Afterword: The Absence of Writing or How I Almost Became a Spy," in *She Tries Her Tongue, Her Silence Softly Breaks* (Middletown, CT: Wesleyan University Press, 2015), pp. 75–91.

19 Katherine McKittrick, "Mathematics Black Life," *The Black Scholar* 44, no. 2 (Summer 2014), p. 18; Dylan Rodríguez, "Black Studies in Impasse," *The Black Scholar* 44, no. 2 (Summer 2014), pp. 37, 47.

20 Saidiya V. Hartman, *Scenes of Subjection: Terror, Slavery, and Self-Making in Nineteenth-Century America* (New York: Oxford University Press, 1997), p. 7.

21 Richard Iton, "Still Life," *Small Axe* 17, no. 1 (March 2013), p. 39.

22 Tau Lewis, quoted in the 52 Walker press release announcing *Vox Populi, Vox Dei*, https://52walker.com/exhibitions/tau-lewis-vox-populi-vox-dei; Iton, "Still Life," p. 39.

Spring to the 1st Magnitude
Yves B. Golden

in the dark of what's over now
gray stars chimed their beginnings
soft-new colors within their mothers
pulsing minor to major—back and forth through Ursa's Harmonia

the thick inky pre-life shouted out shards
thorns
splintering through the vacuum sprouting seeds

lenticular dinging stars
starts
springs
in the milky voids between filaments
horning plenty
escorted through matter and silence
in the folds of sateen pedals

the mothering TAUBIS
bearing overflowing asterisms
lay their shells on the banks of cold flows
to dance in heat and time
to liquify The Truth
in the mouths of young homunculi

circadian in the void
golden
musically blooming life
rouging
conducting the young dinging of infinity
holographic

their lyre-bodies strum into familiar forms to reflect all worlds
all minds
like a cathedral—
their webbed filament architecture
joins The Truth pulsing with the eldest Black tone
to Harmonia.

PLATES

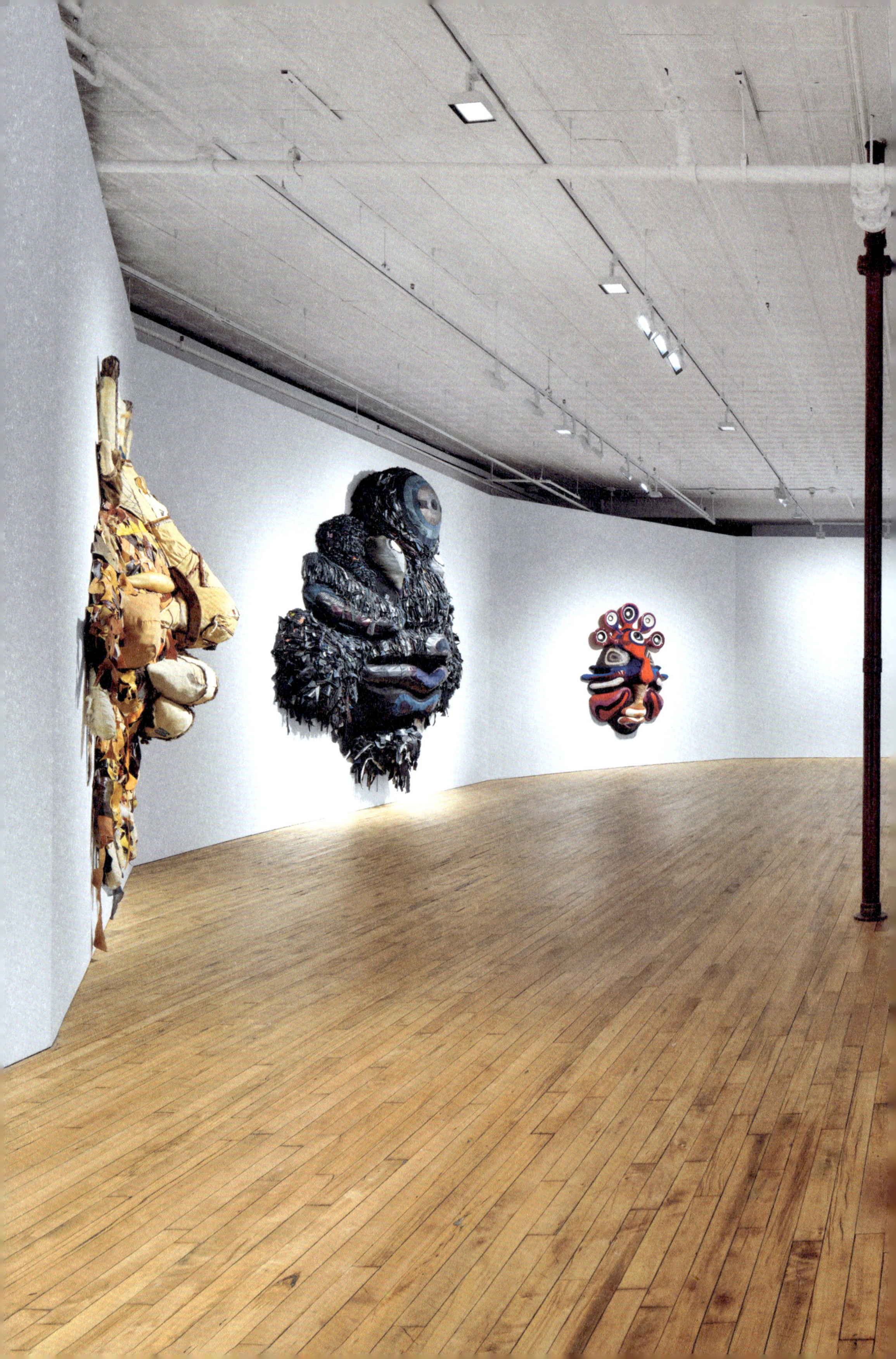

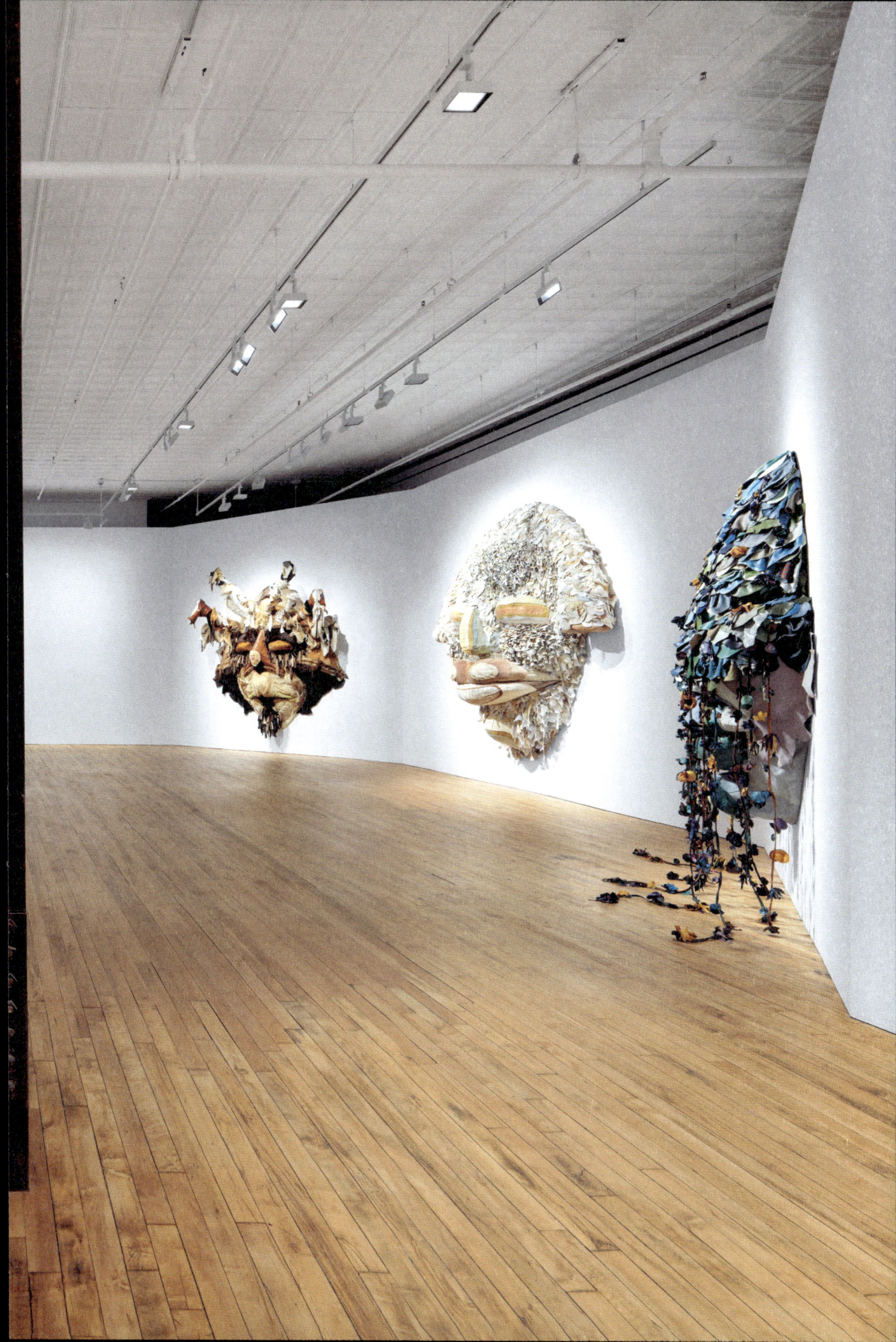

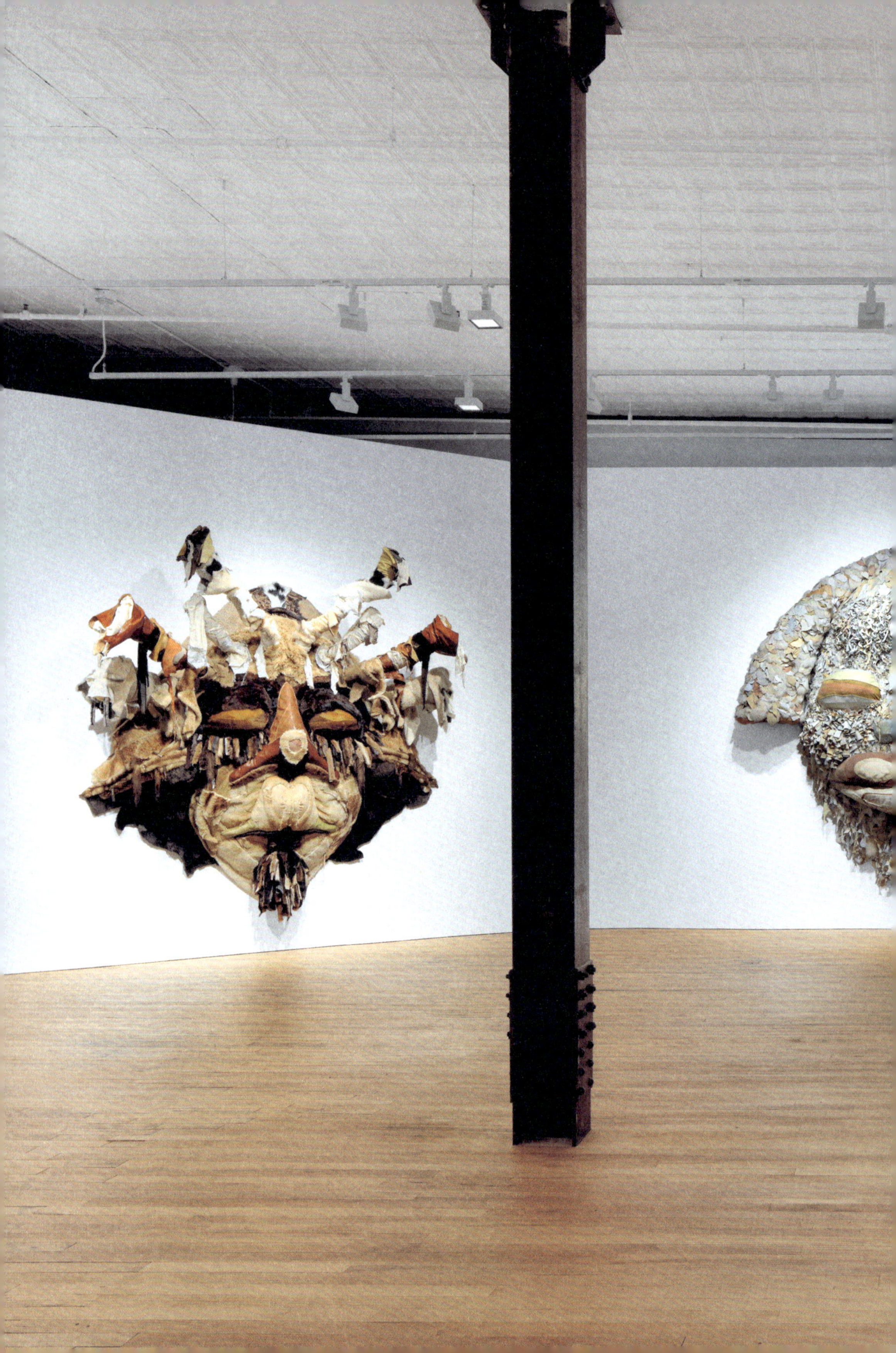

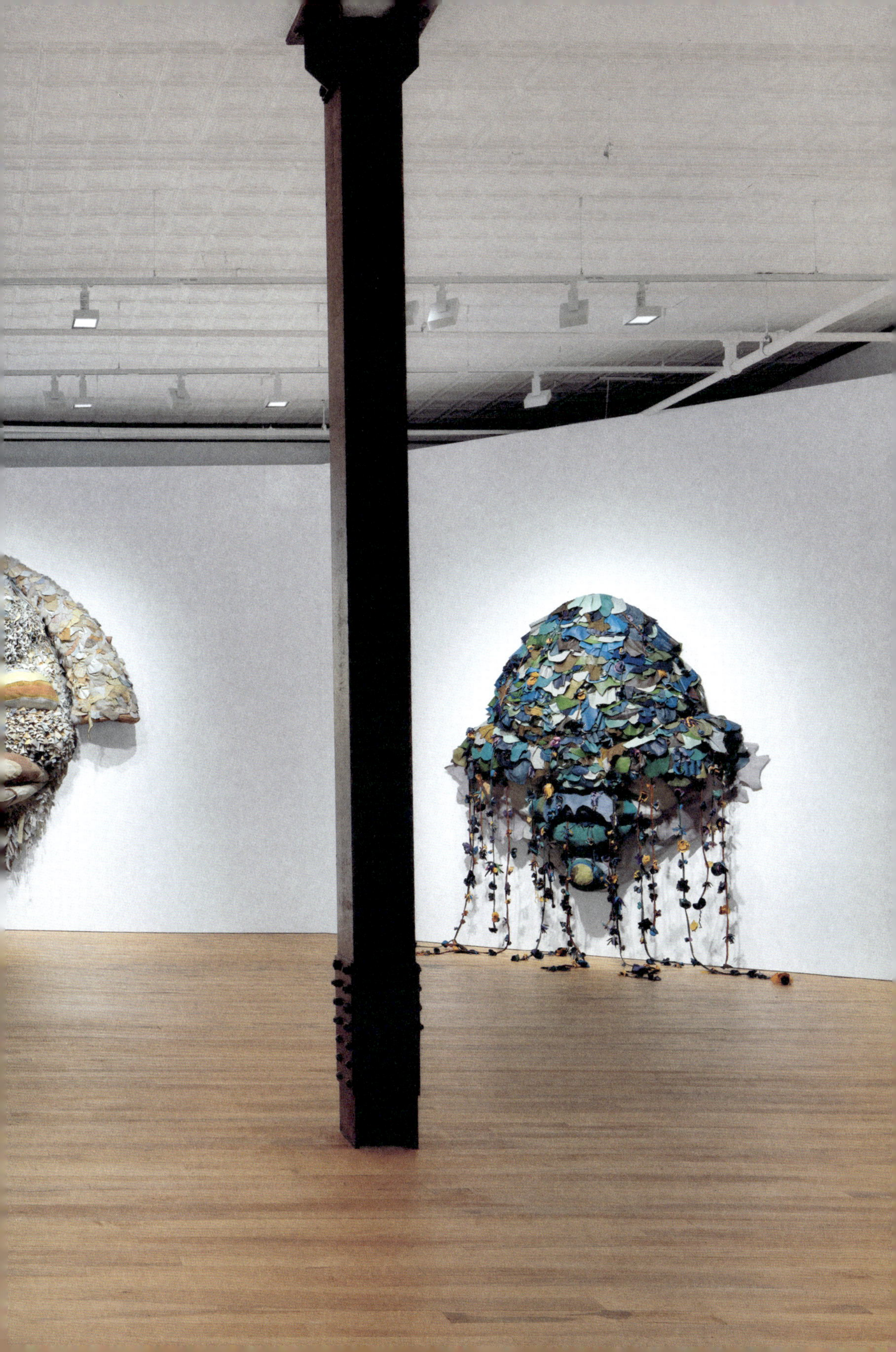

Resurrector, 2022
Steel, enamel paint, repurposed leather, fur, suede, shearling, coat linings, silk, chalk
pastel, organic cotton twill, and coated nylon thread
116 × 110 ½ × 37 inches | 294.6 × 280.7 × 94 cm

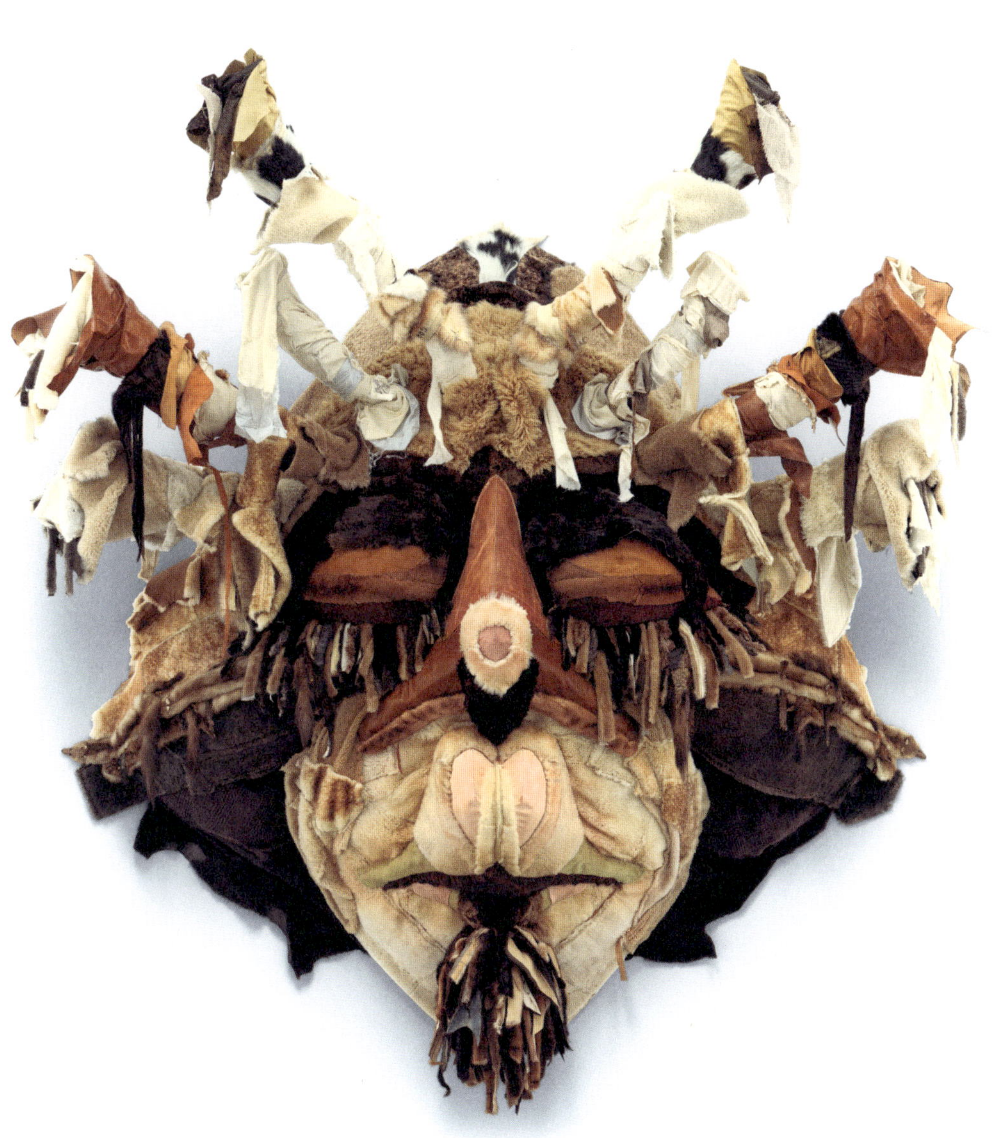

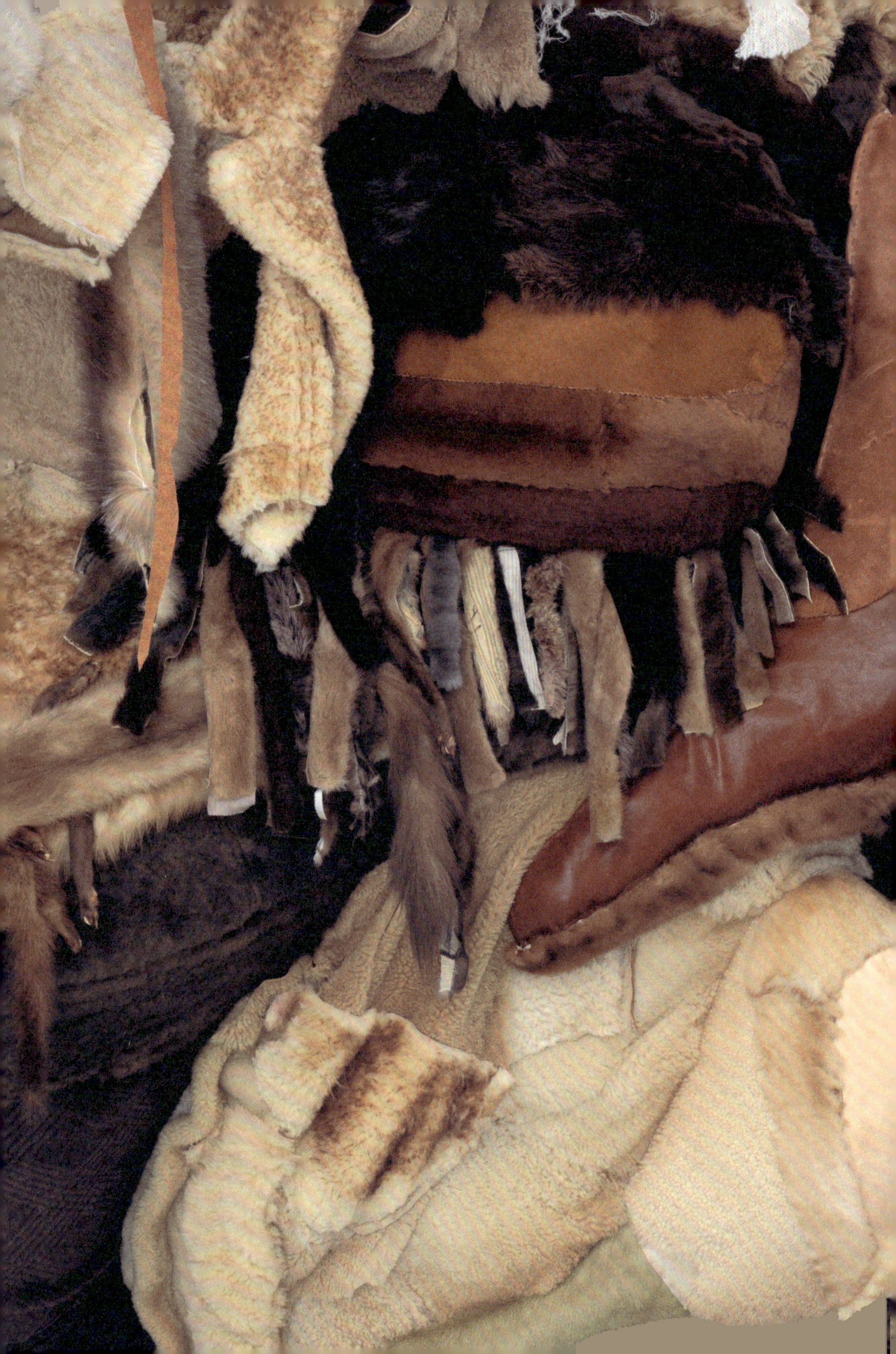

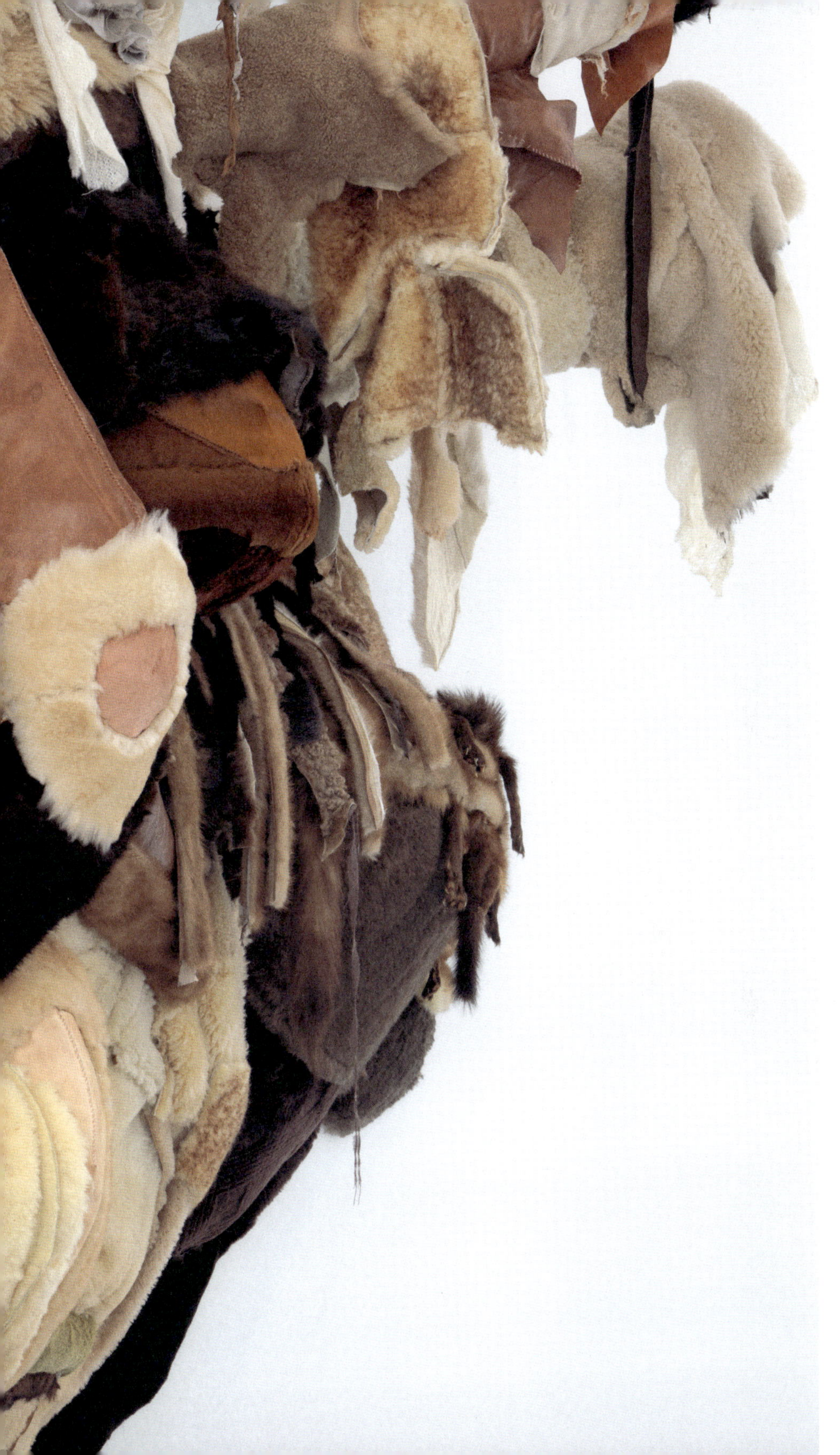

Ivory Gate, 2022
Steel, enamel paint, acrylic paint and finisher, repurposed leather, suede, fur, shearling, snakeskin, shells, fossilized teeth, organic cotton twill, and coated nylon thread
124 ½ × 137 ⅛ × 37 ½ inches | 316.2 × 348.3 × 95.3 cm

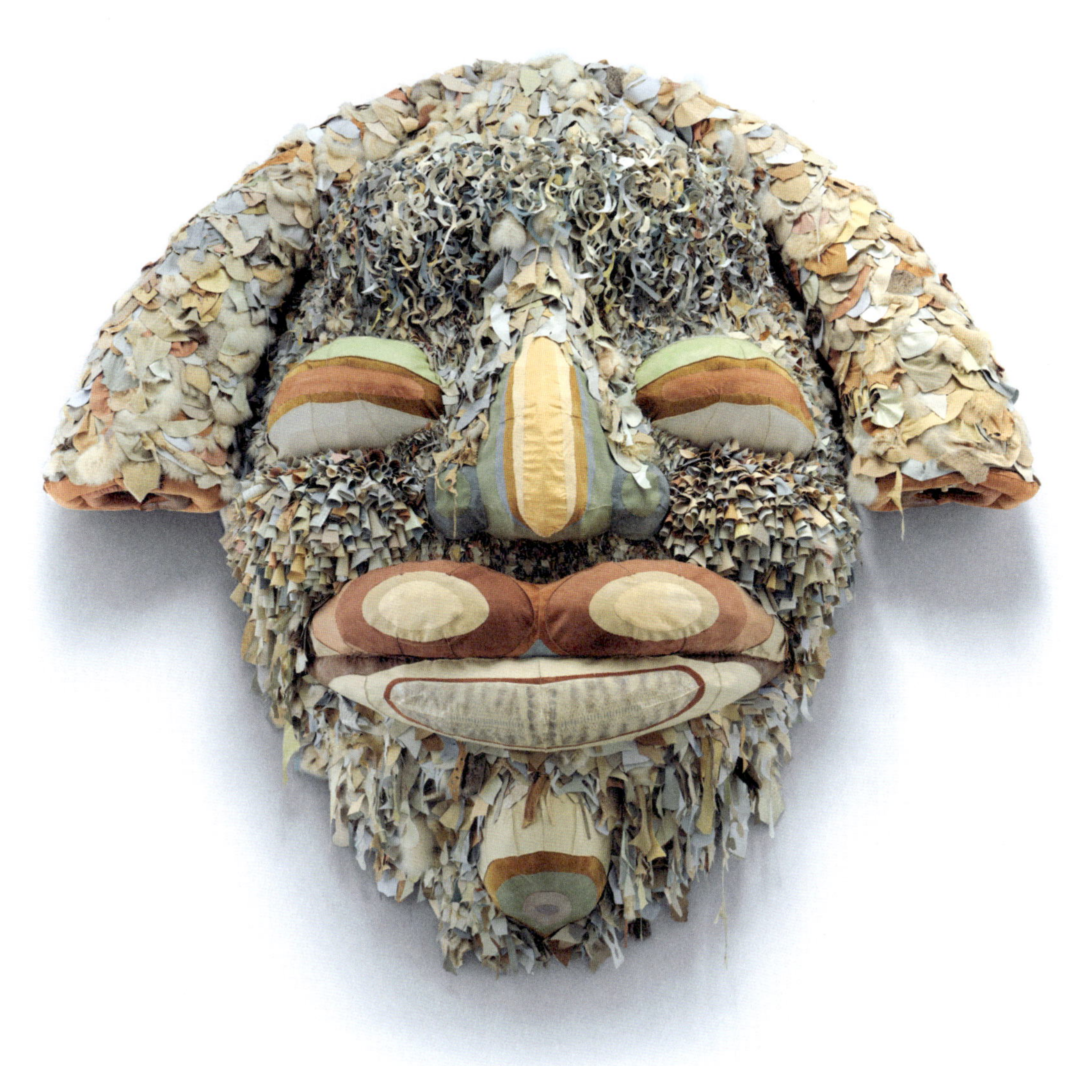

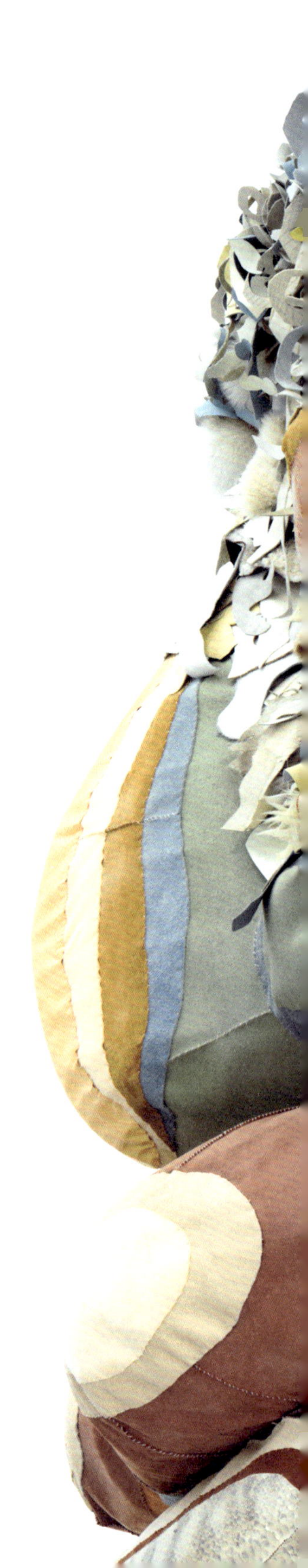

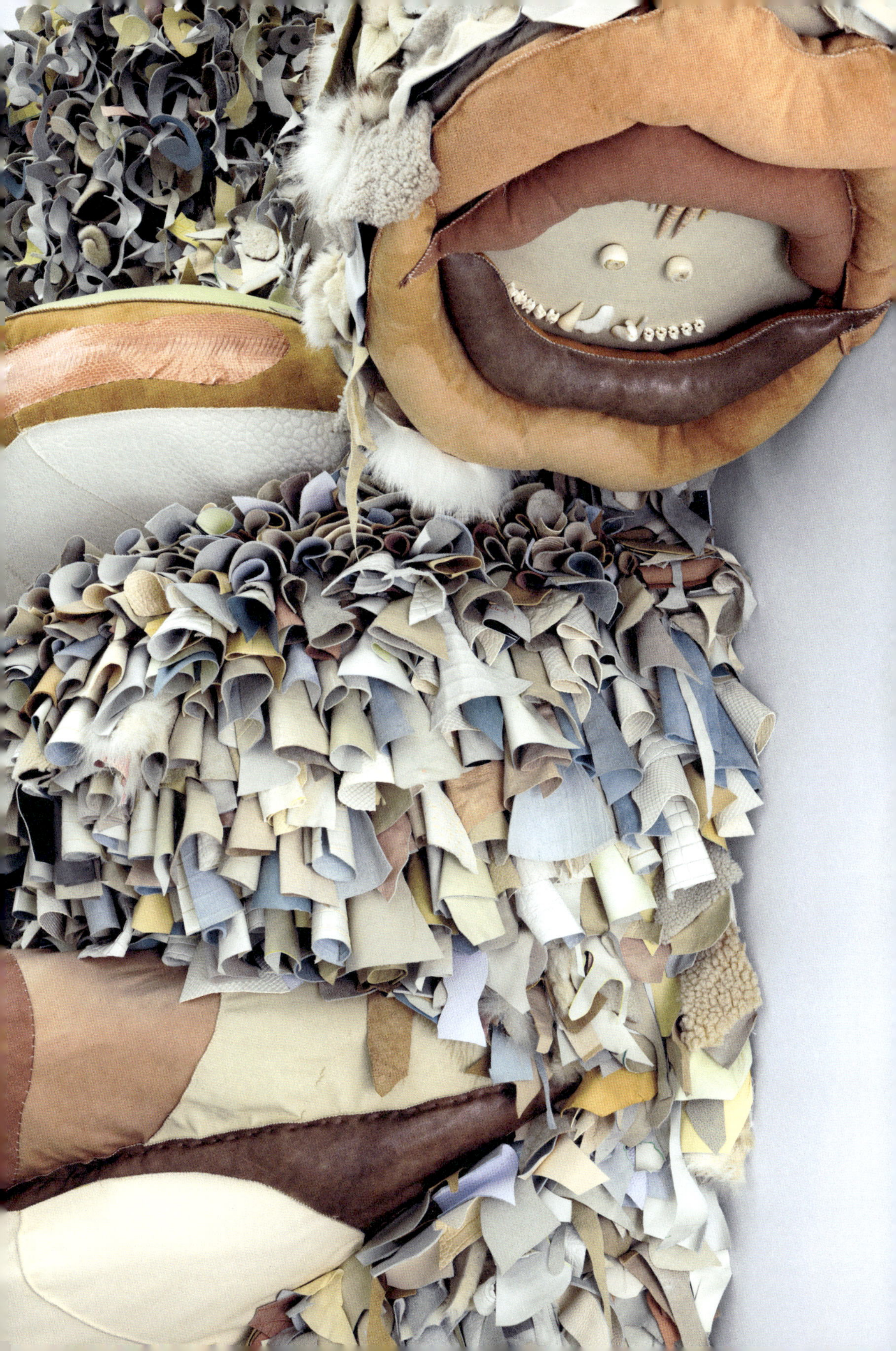

Saint Mozelle, 2022
Steel, enamel paint, acrylic paint and finisher, repurposed leather and suede, organic
cotton twill, and coated nylon thread
113 ¾ × 95 ¼ × 59 inches | 288.9 × 241.9 × 149.9 cm

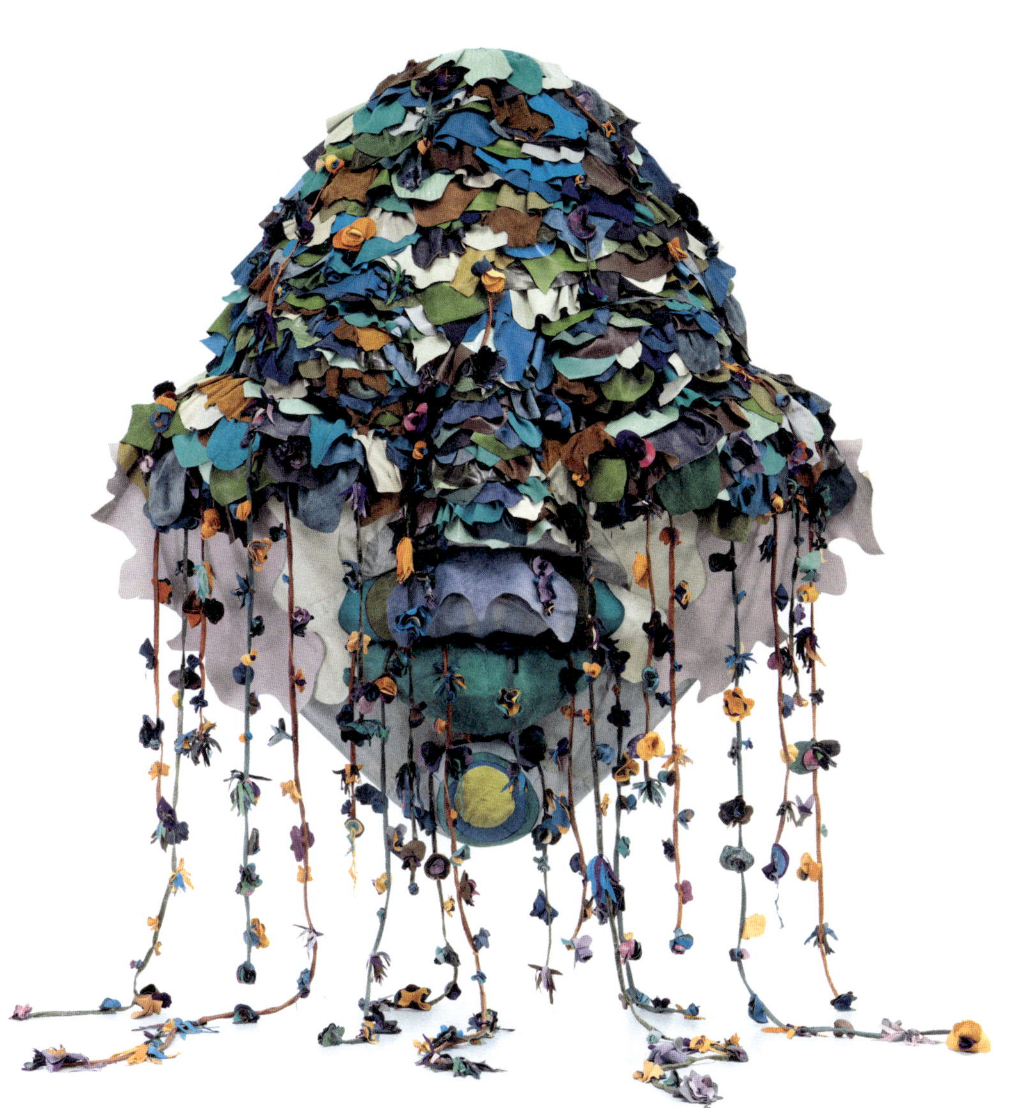

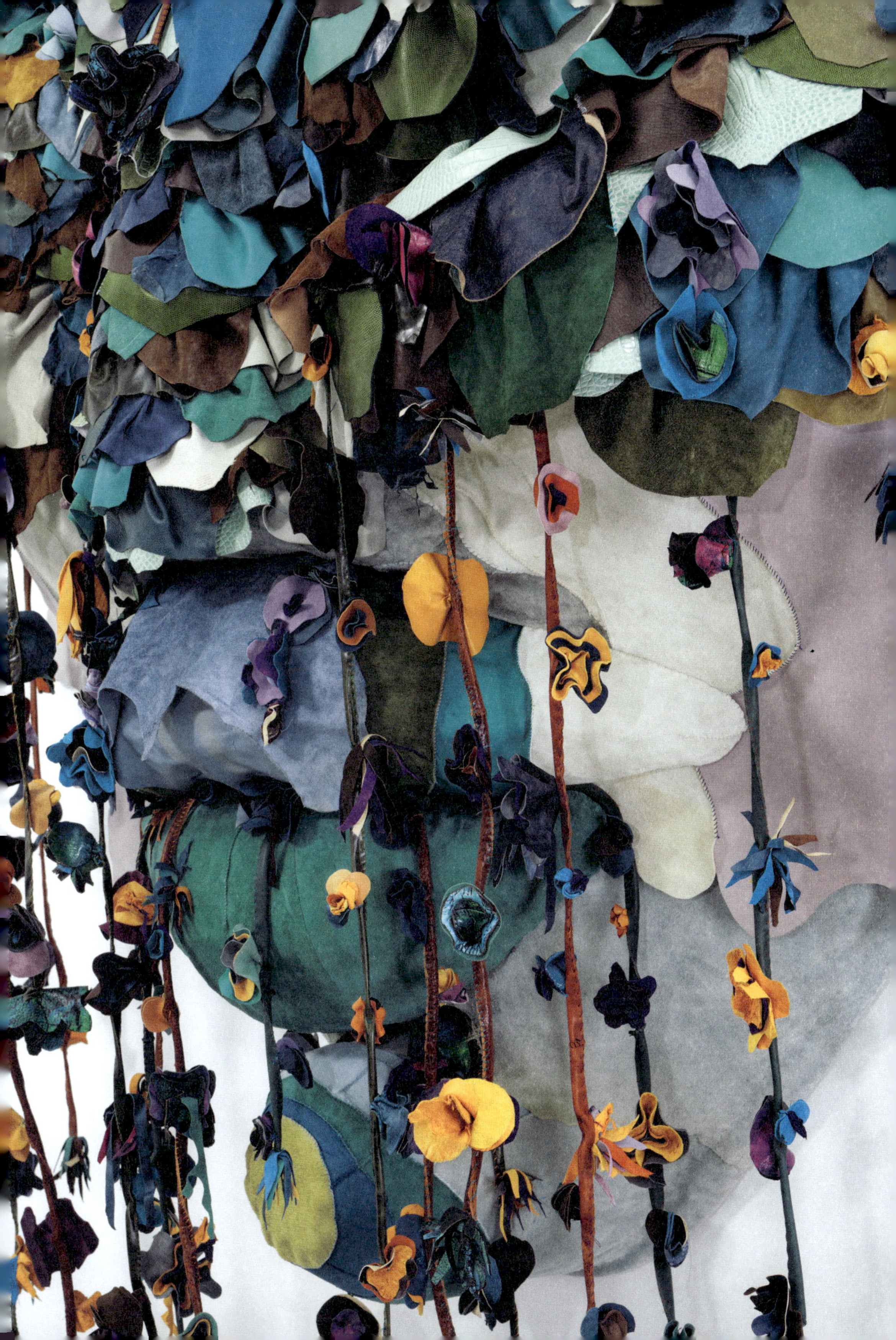

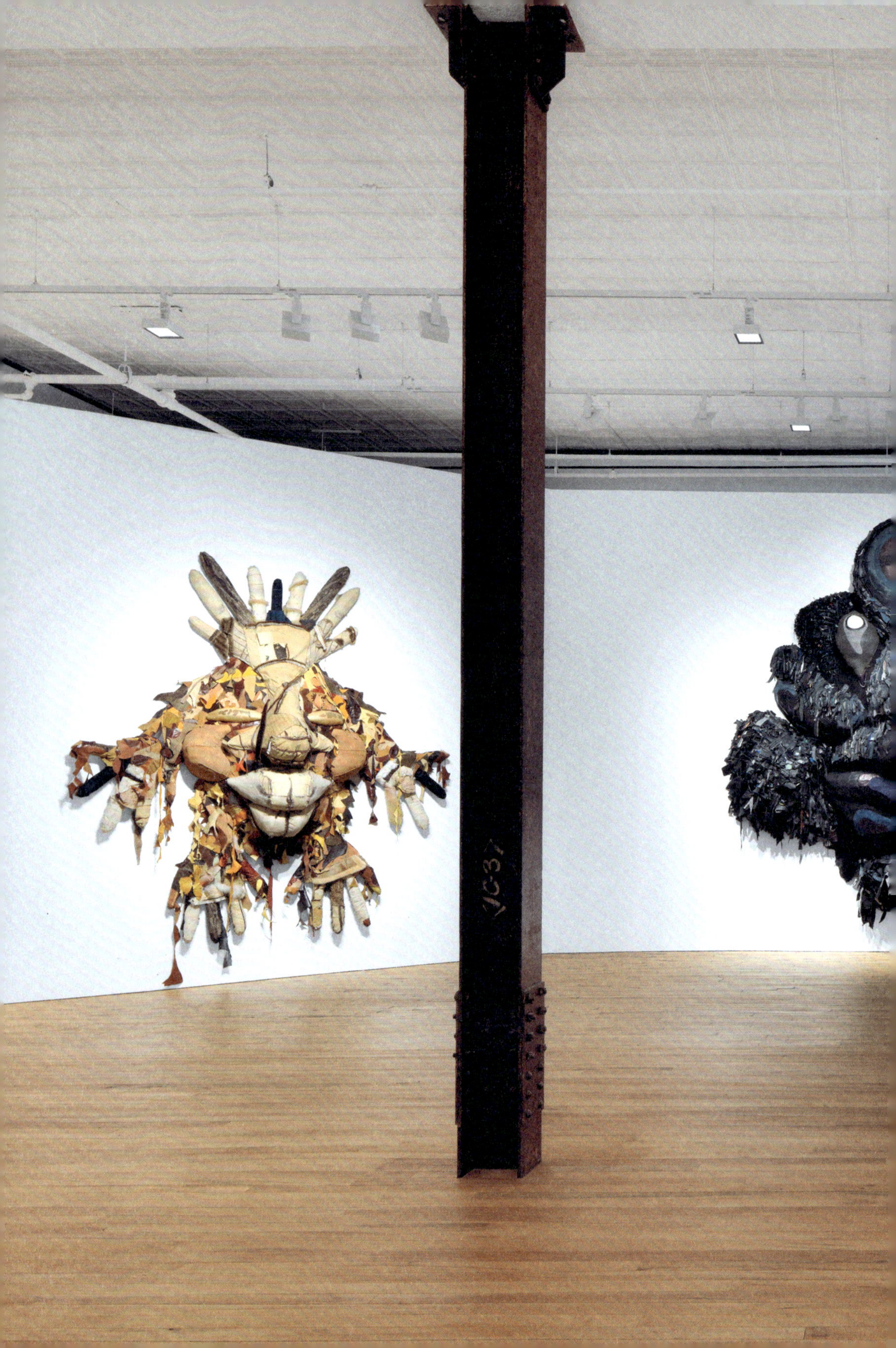

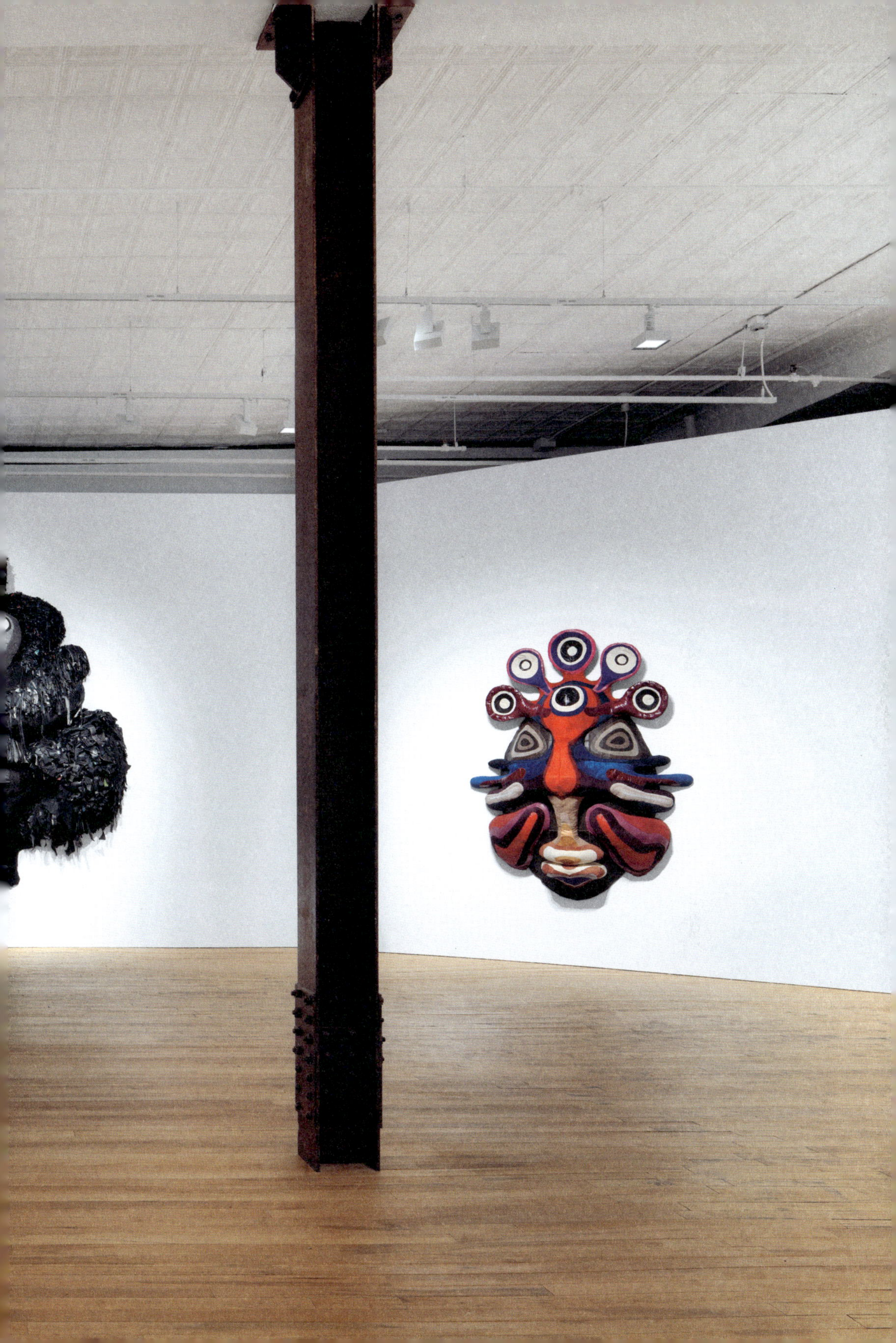

Mater Dei, 2022
Steel, enamel paint, repurposed leather, fur, shearling, suede, rawhide,
organic cotton twill, and coated nylon thread
134 × 113 ⅜ × 31 inches | 340.4 × 288 × 78.7 cm

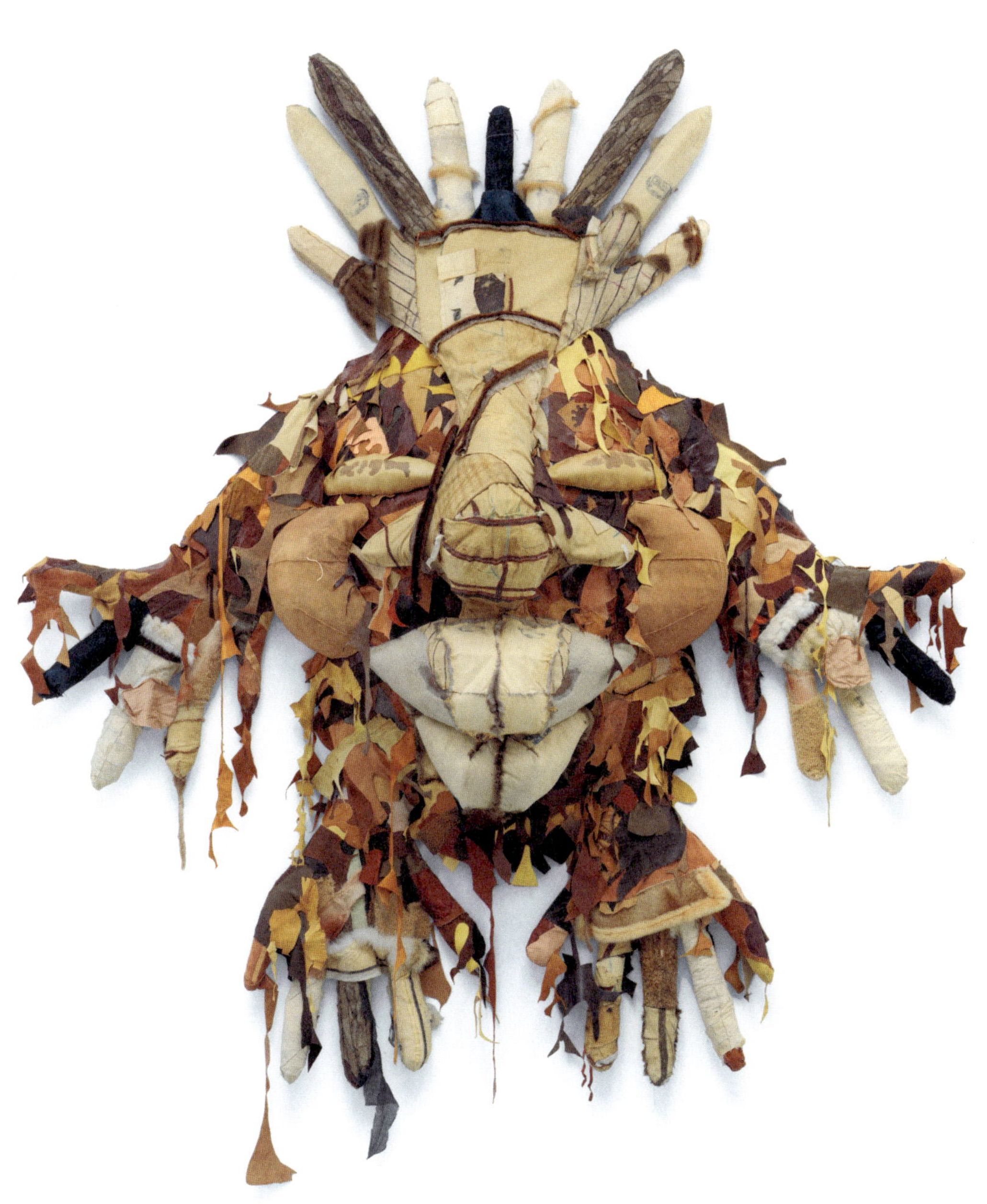

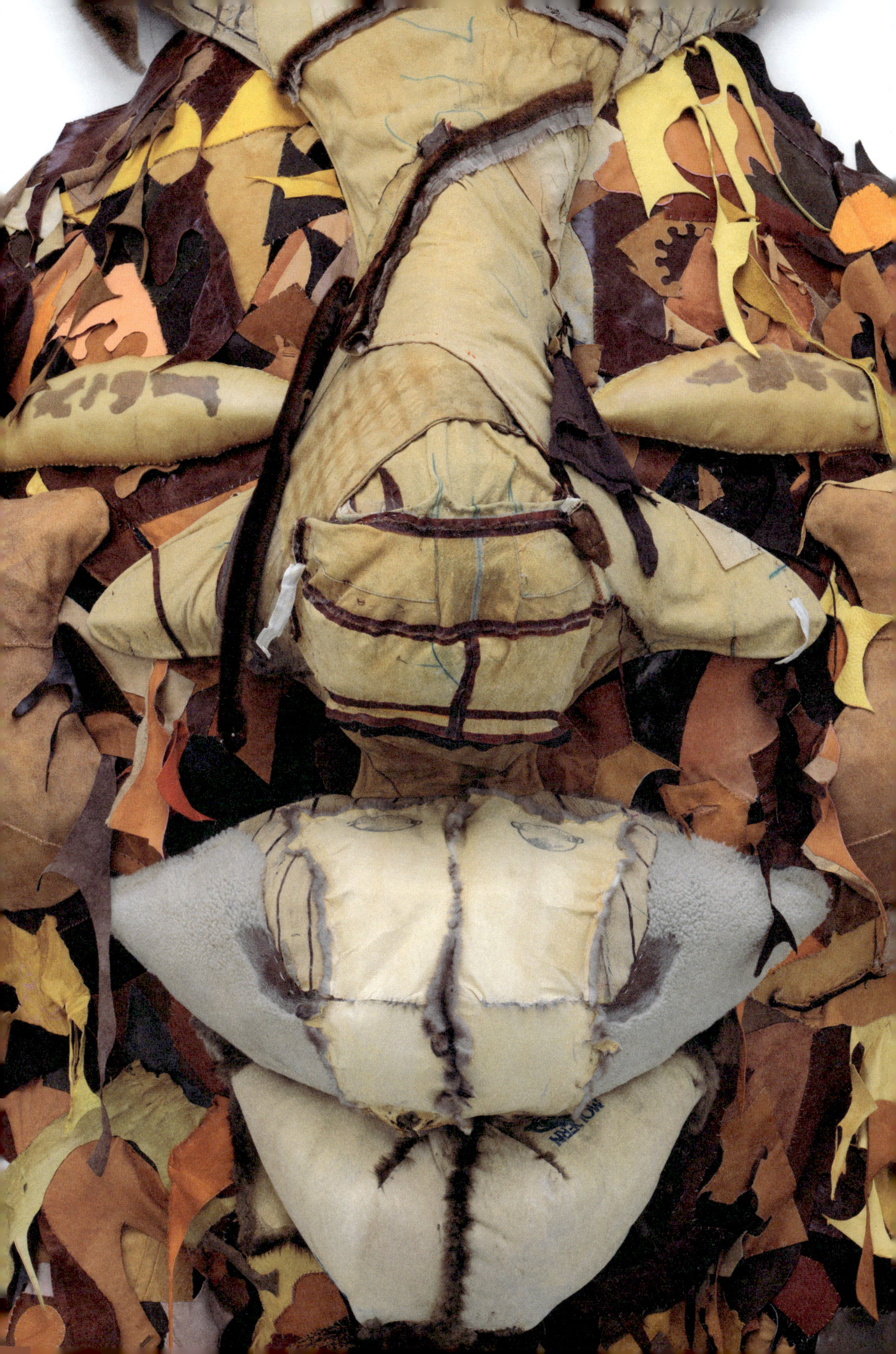

Trident, 2022
Steel, enamel paint, acrylic paint and finisher, repurposed leather, shearling, shagreen, fur, suede, snakeskin, organic cotton twill, and coated nylon thread
159 × 135 ¼ × 37 ¾ inches | 403.9 × 343.5 × 95.9 cm

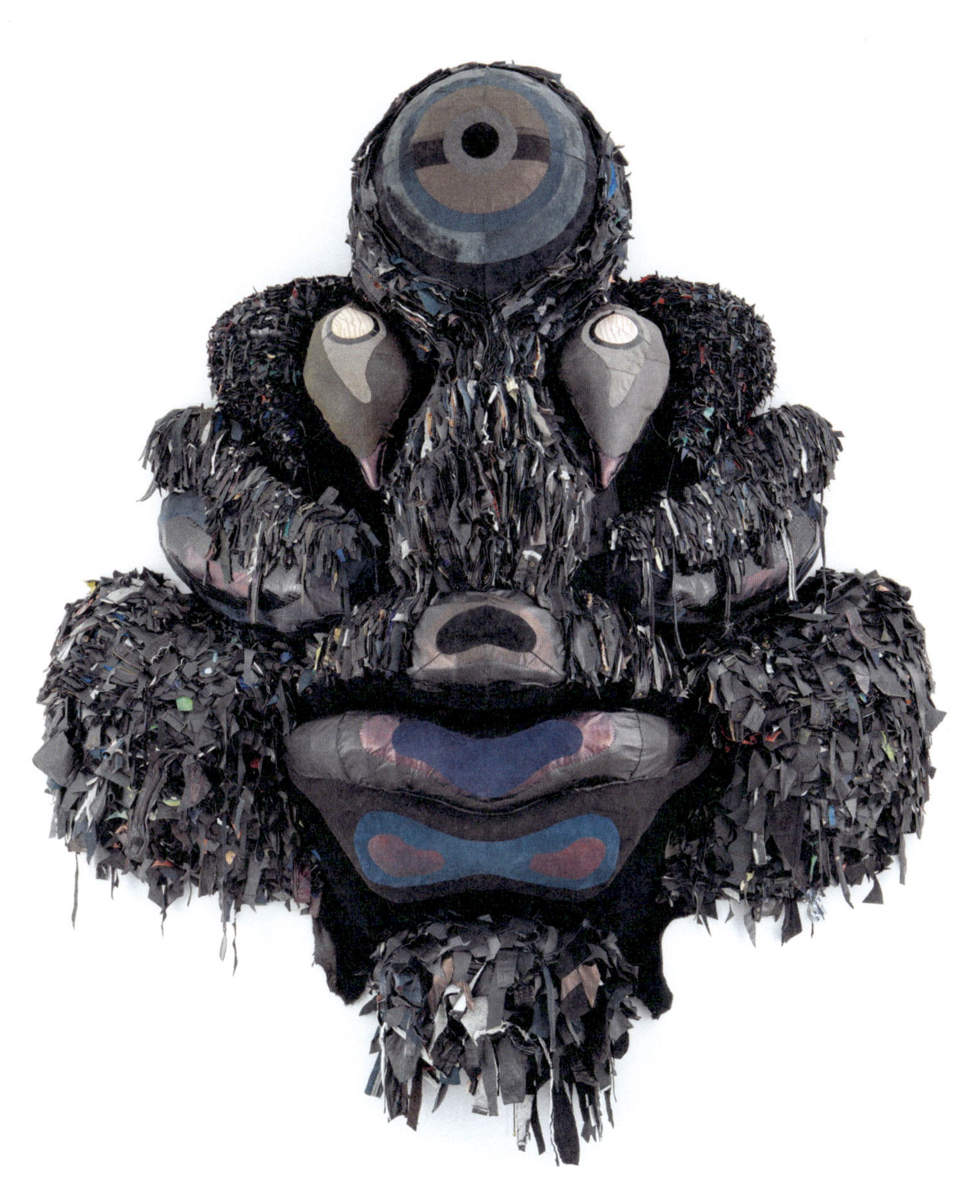

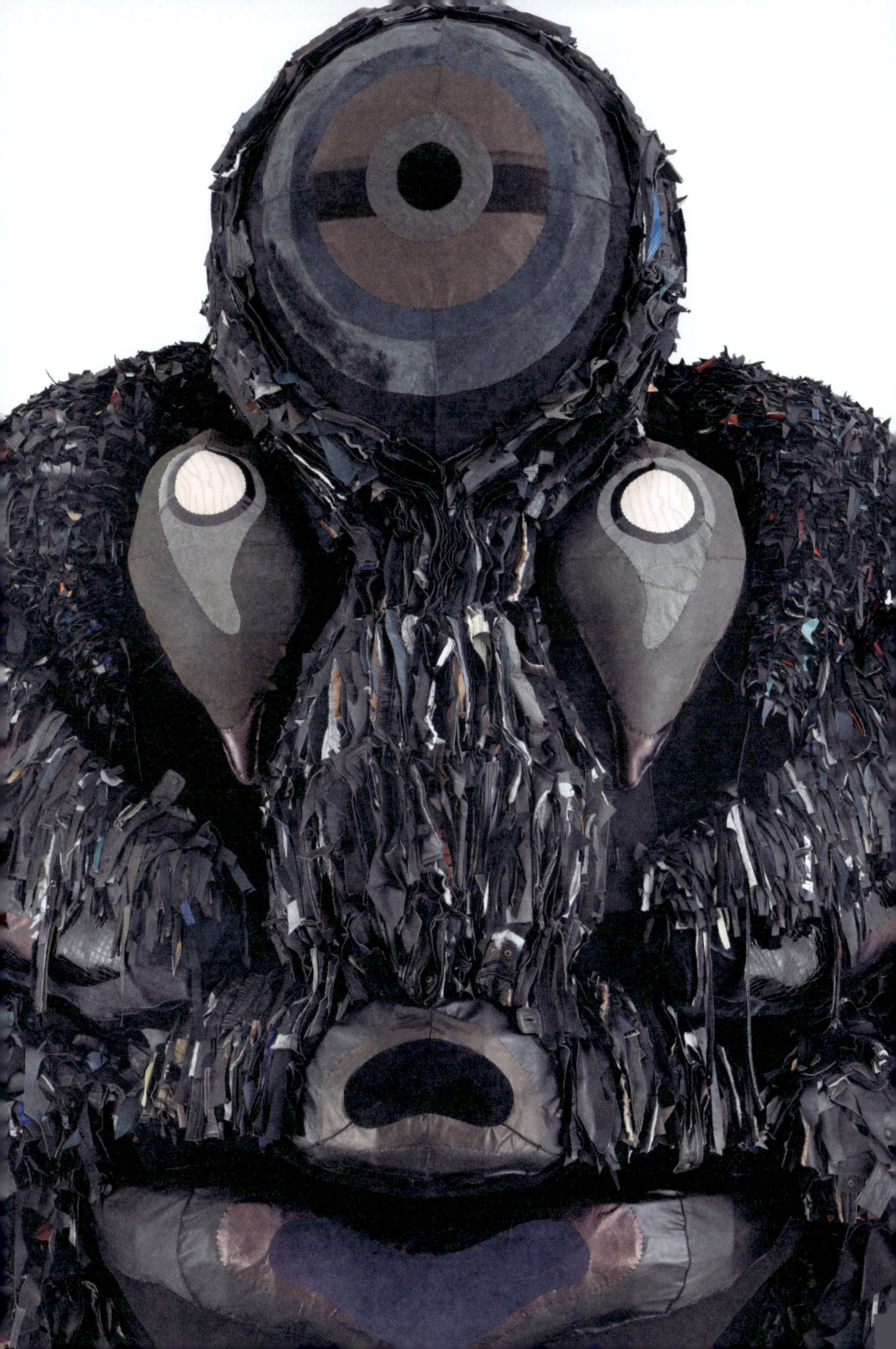

Homonoia, 2022
Steel, enamel paint, acrylic paint and finisher, repurposed leather and suede, organic
cotton twill, and coated nylon thread
88 ½ × 68 × 26 ¼ inches | 224.8 × 172.7 × 66.7 cm

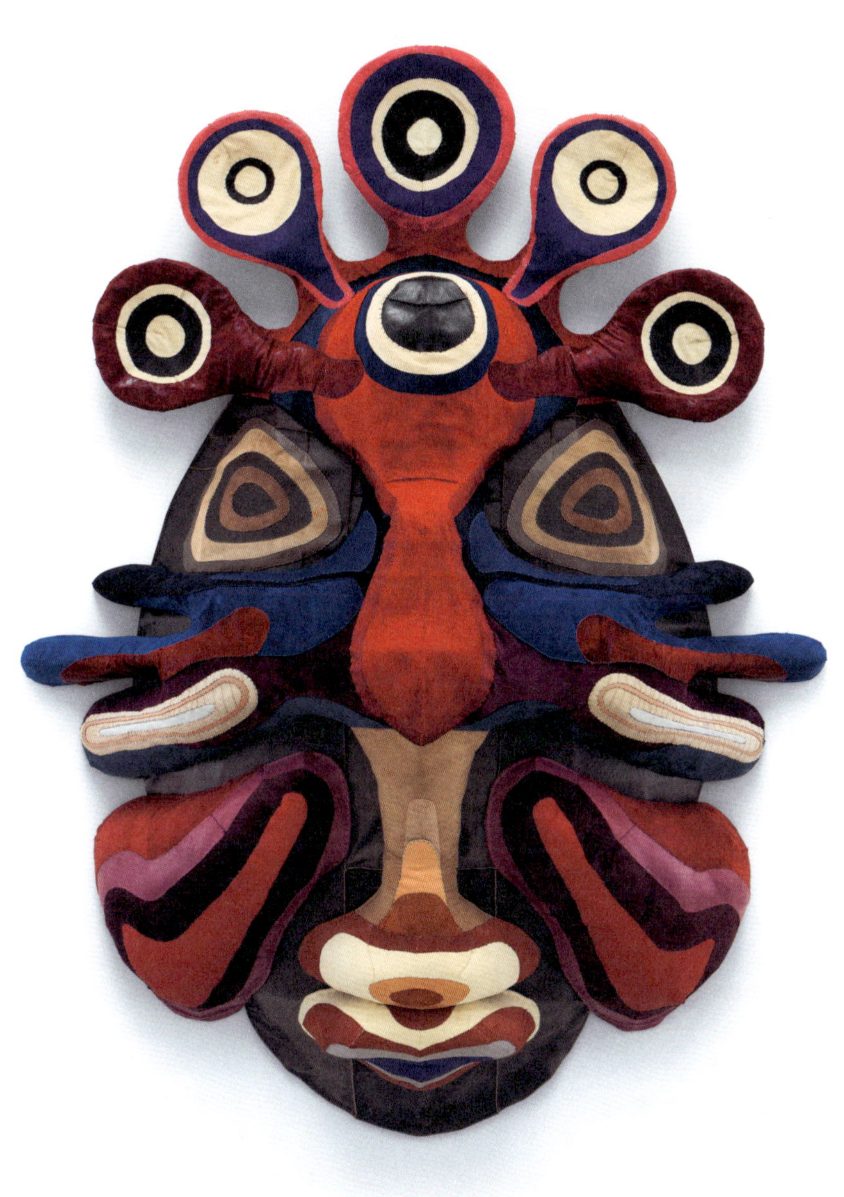

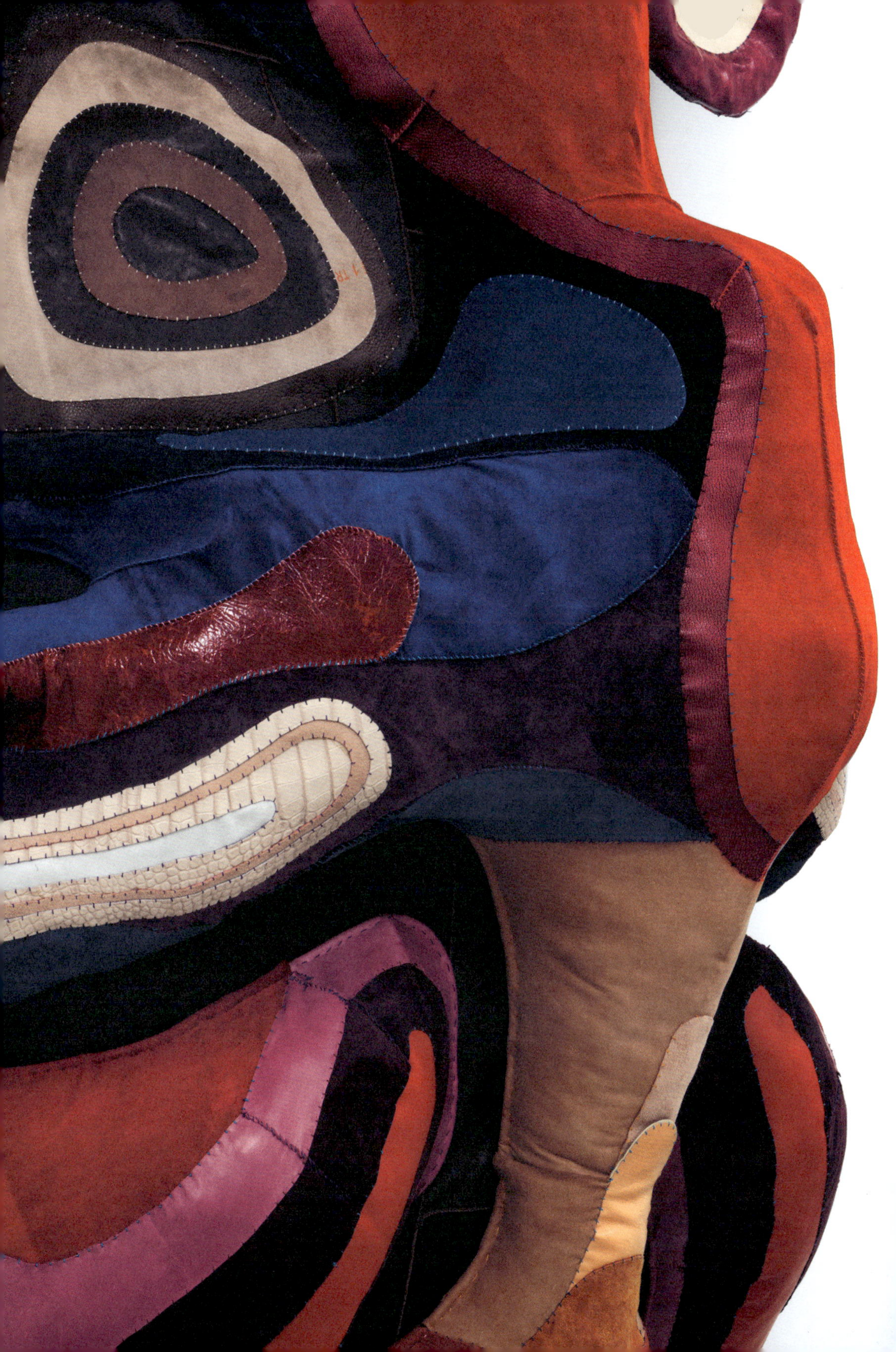

Homonoia, 2022
Steel, enamel paint, acrylic paint and finisher, repurposed leather and suede, organic
cotton twill, and coated nylon thread
44 × 68 × 66 ½ inches | 111.8 × 172.7 × 168.9 cm

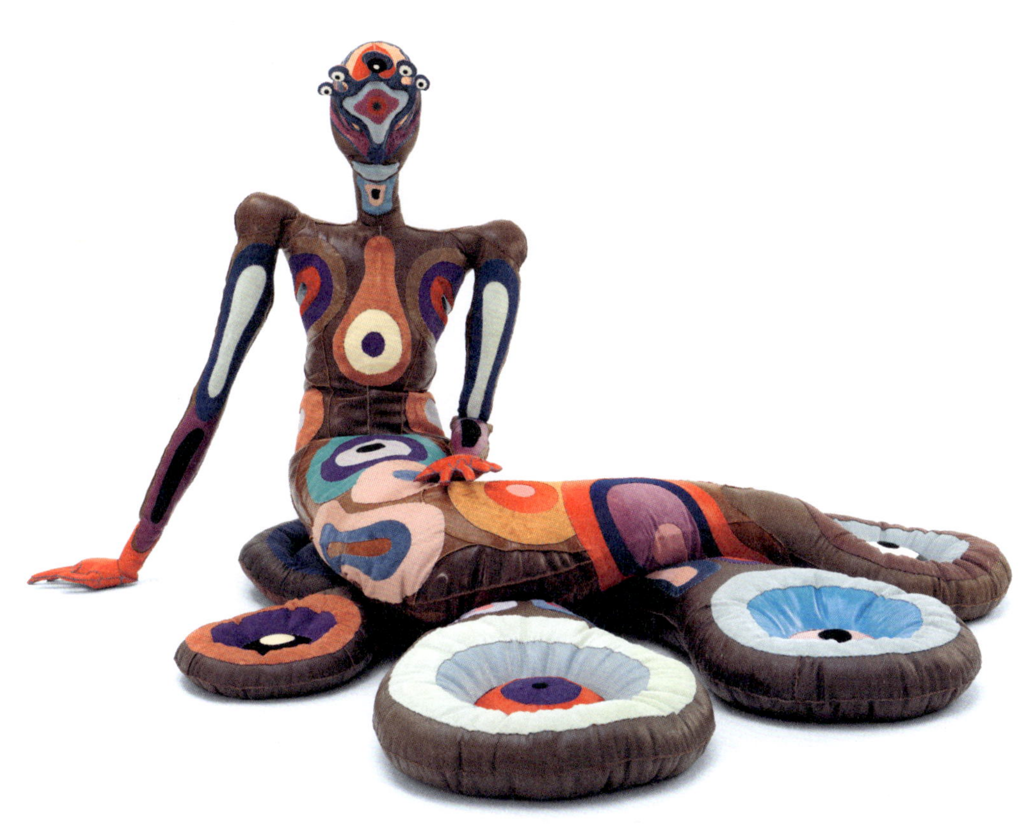

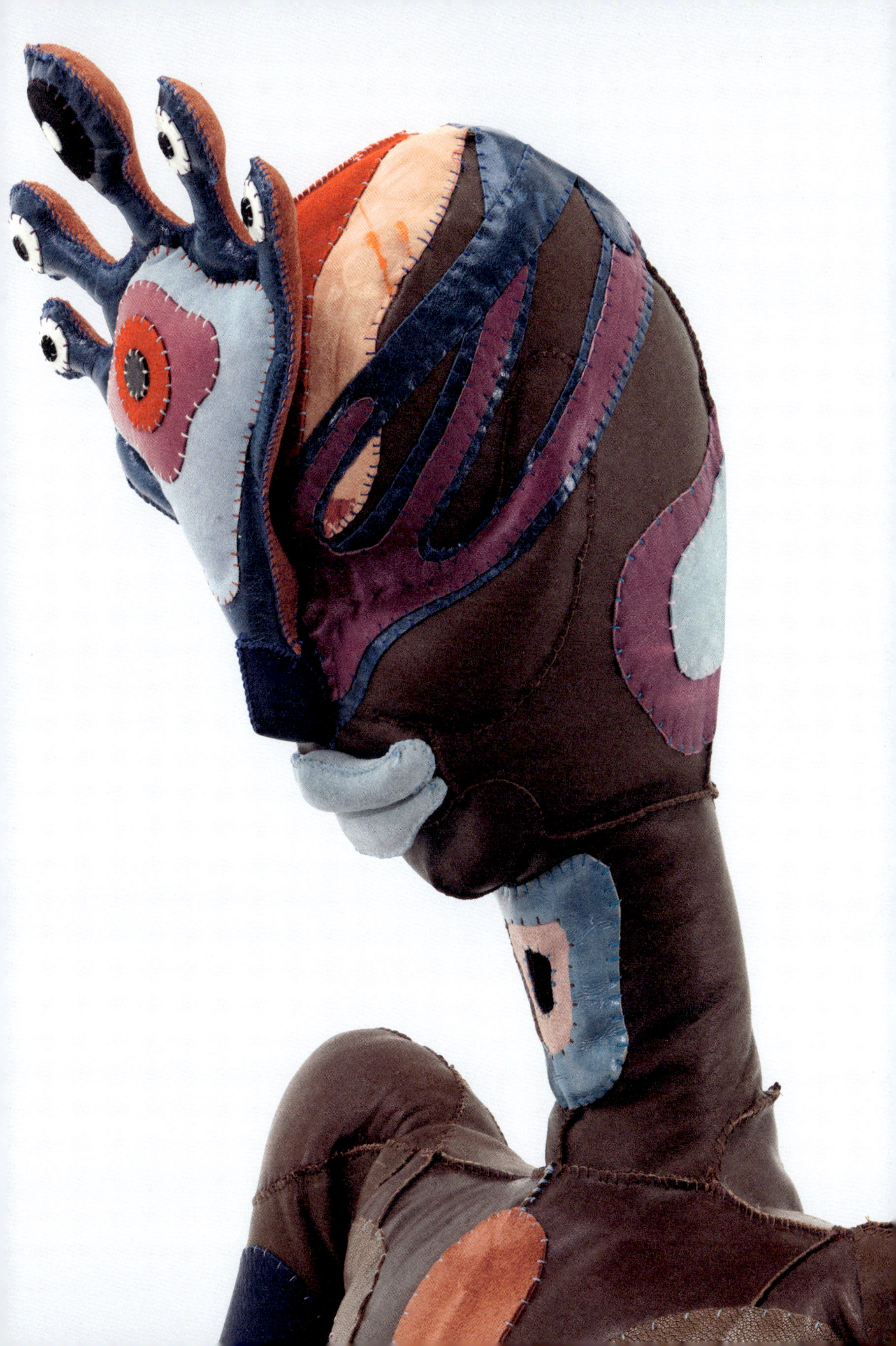

Resurrector, 2022
Steel, enamel paint, repurposed leather, fur, suede, shearling, coat linings, silk, chalk
pastel, organic cotton twill, and coated nylon thread
55 × 57 ½ × 63 inches | 139.7 × 147 × 160 cm

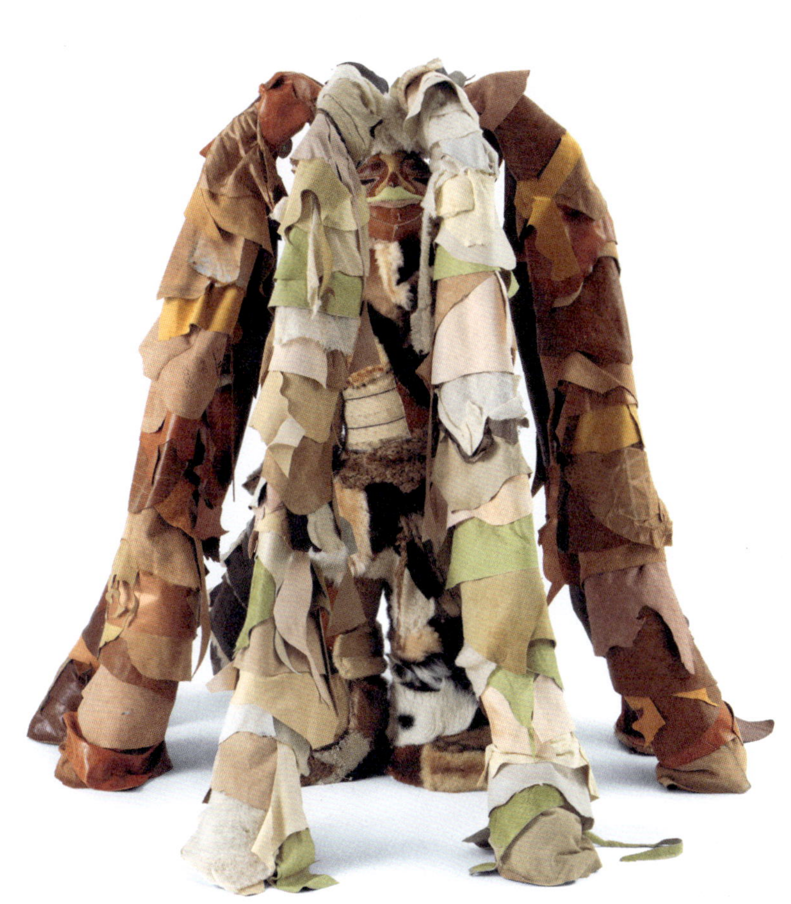

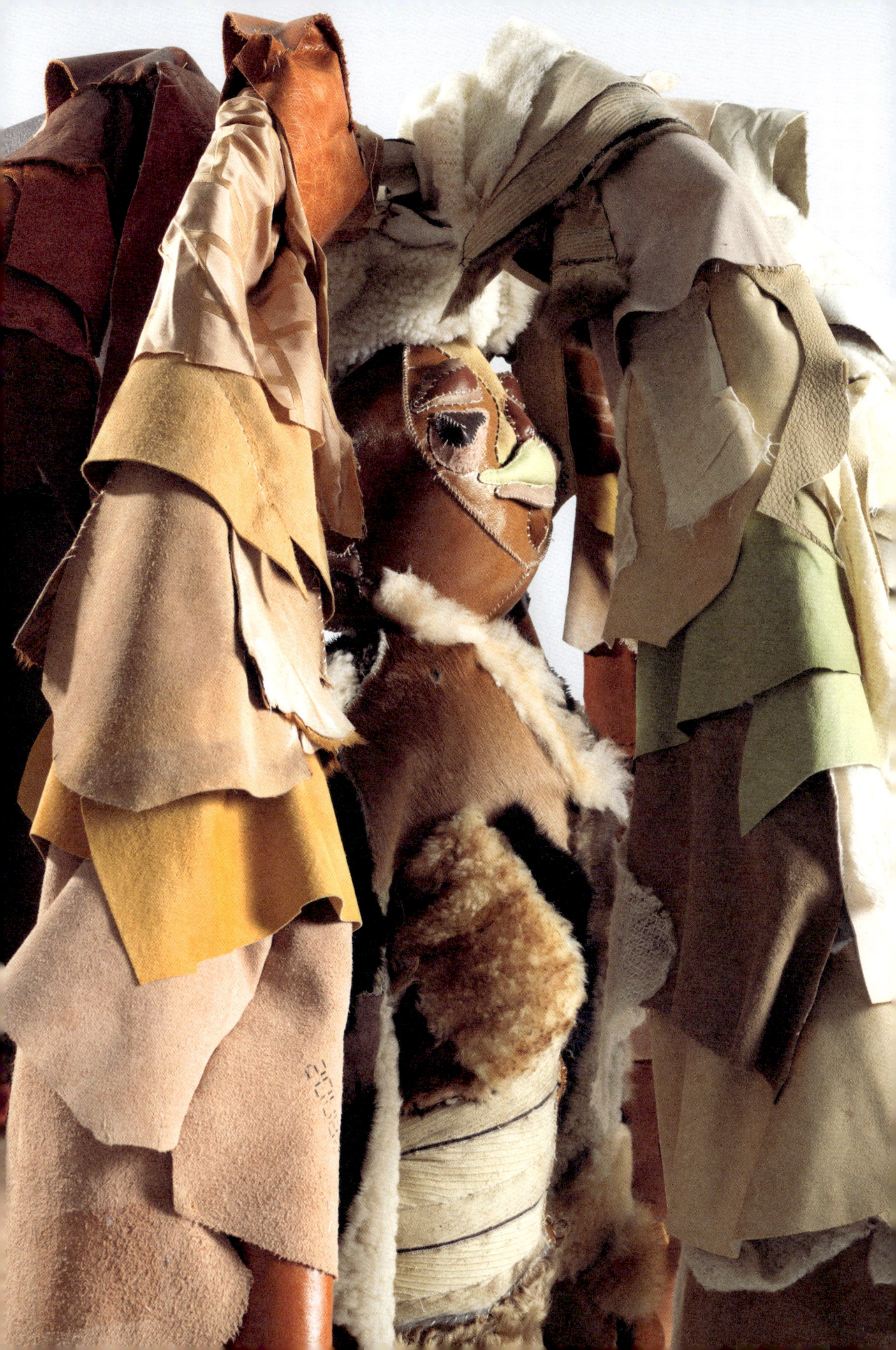

Saint Mozelle, 2022
Steel, enamel paint, acrylic paint and finisher, repurposed leather and suede, organic
cotton twill, and coated nylon thread
75 ½ × 77 × 67 inches | 191.8 × 195.6 × 170.2 cm

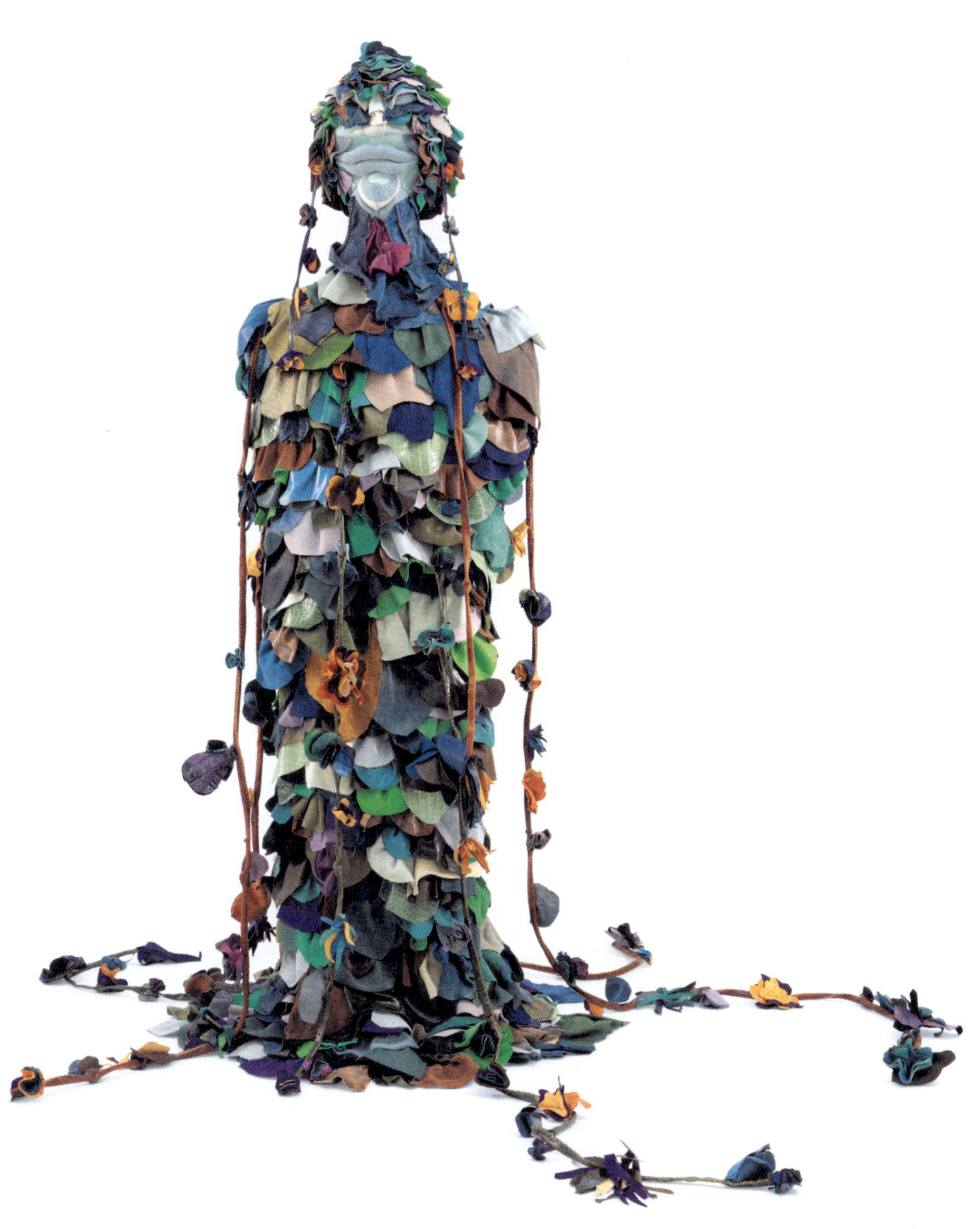

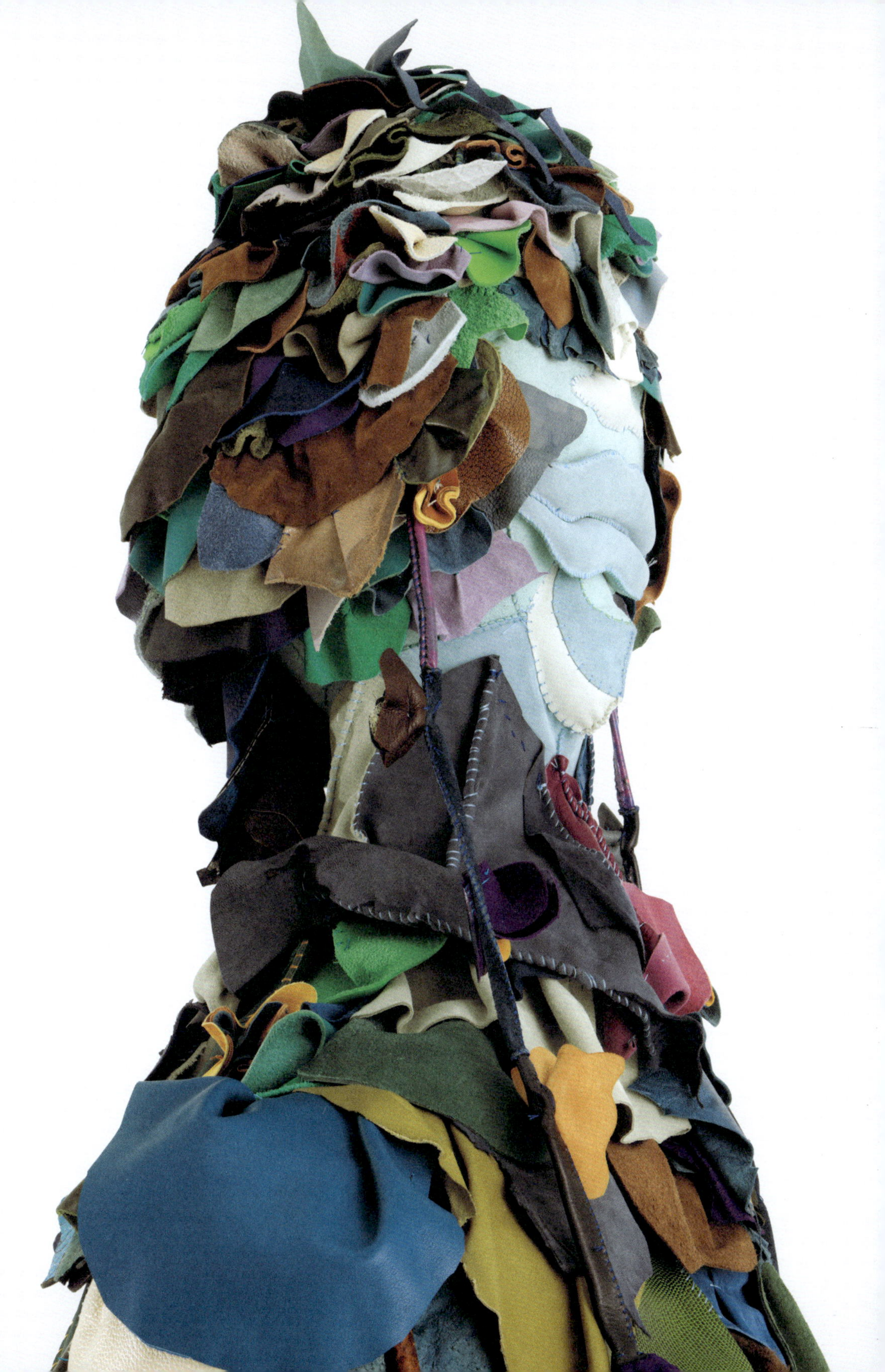

Trident, 2022
Steel, enamel paint, acrylic paint and finisher, repurposed leather, fur, suede, shearling, shagreen, snakeskin, clamshells, organic cotton twill, and coated nylon thread
39 ¼ × 44 × 36 inches | 99.7 × 111.8 × 91.4 cm

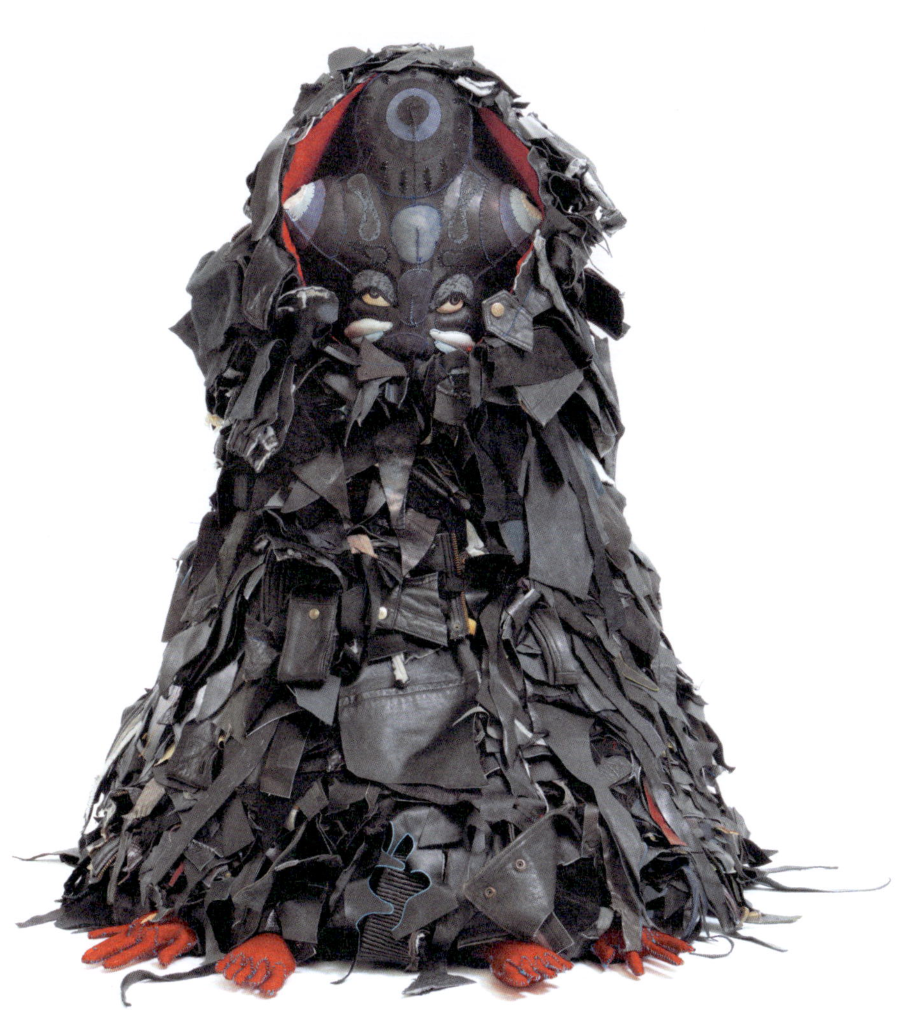

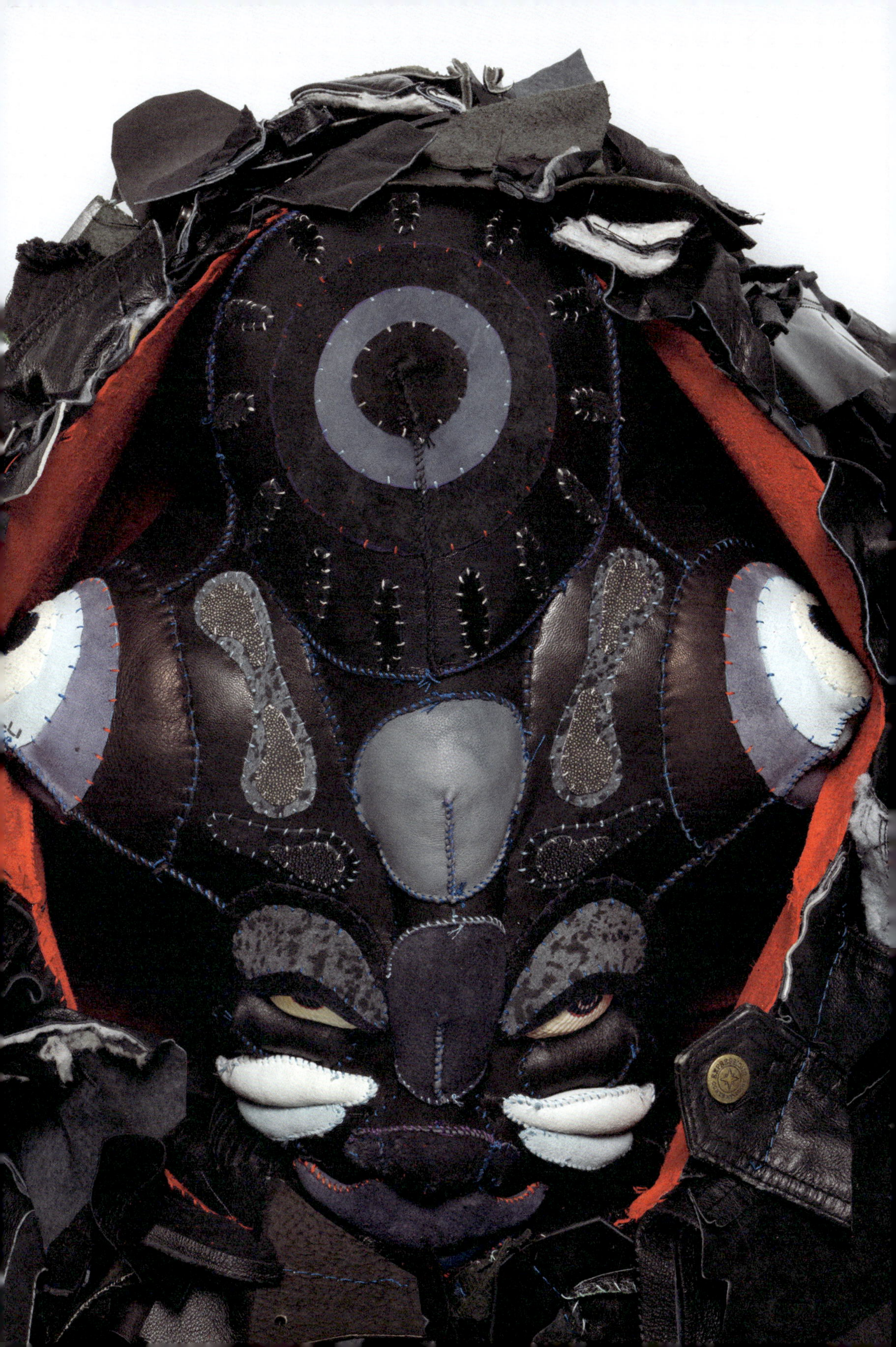

Ivory Gate, 2022
Steel, enamel paint, acrylic paint and finisher, repurposed leather, fur, suede, shearling,
conch shells, snakeskin, chalk pastel, organic cotton twill, and coated nylon thread
61 ¼ × 59 ½ × 30 inches | 155.6 × 151.1 × 76.2 cm

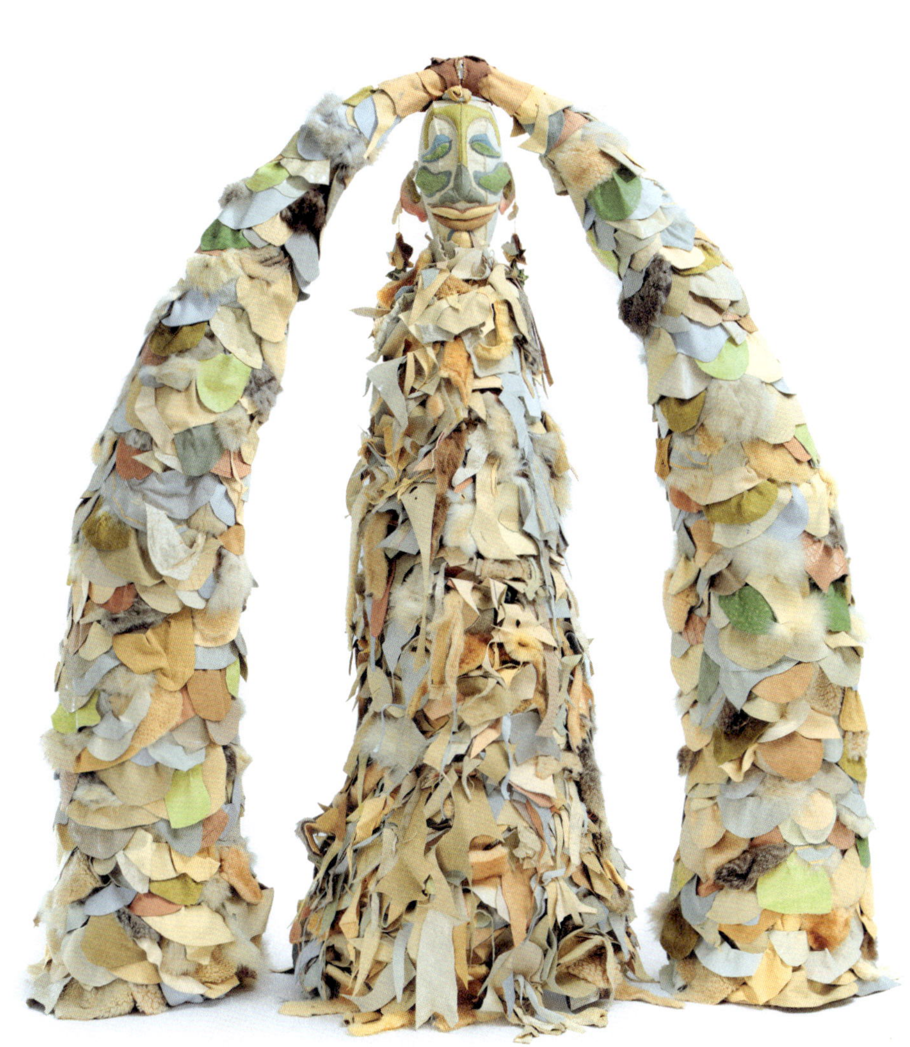

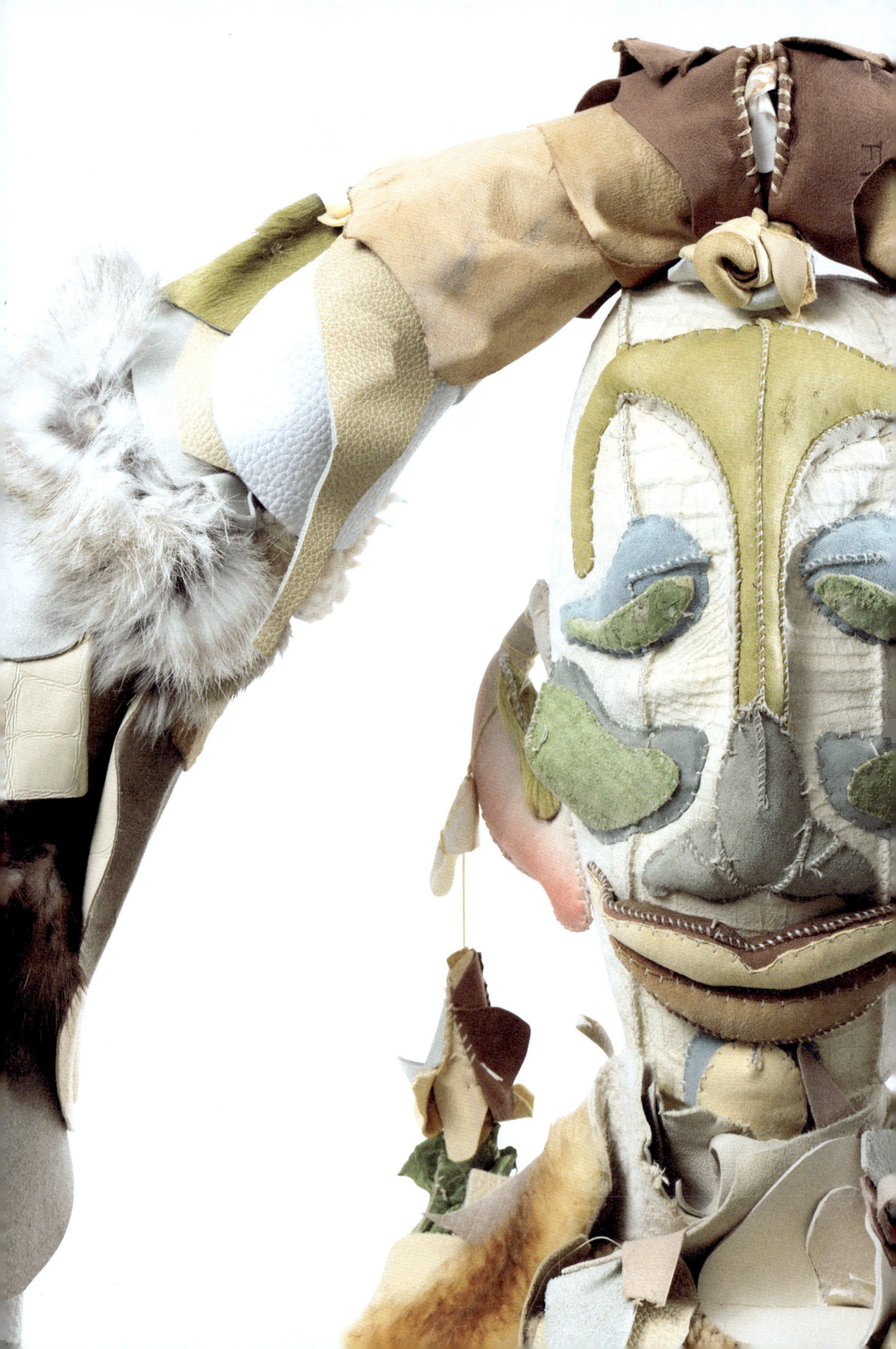

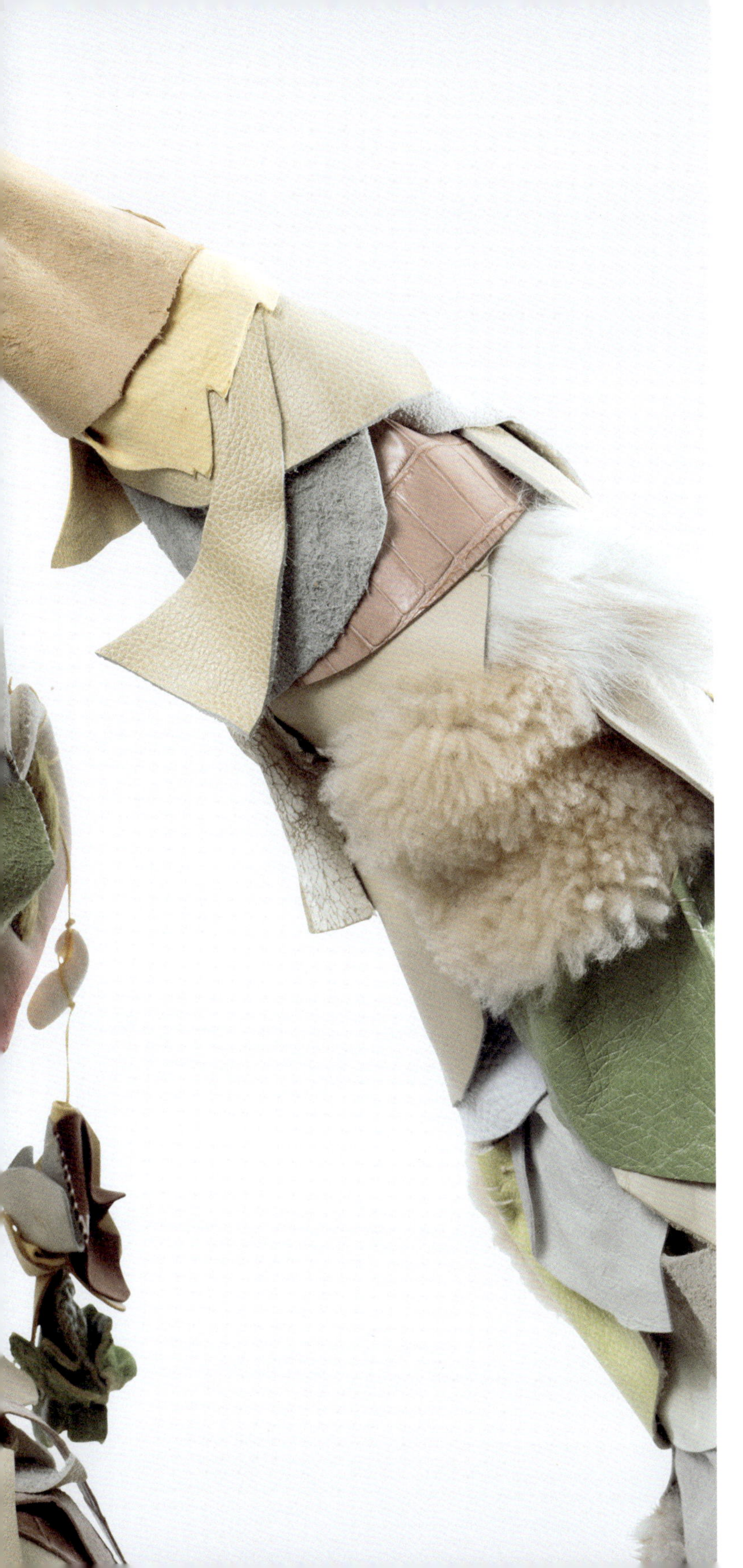

Pages 71–95
Preparatory studies, 2021–2022
Colored pencil, ink, and fabric on paper; 27 works
Dimensions variable

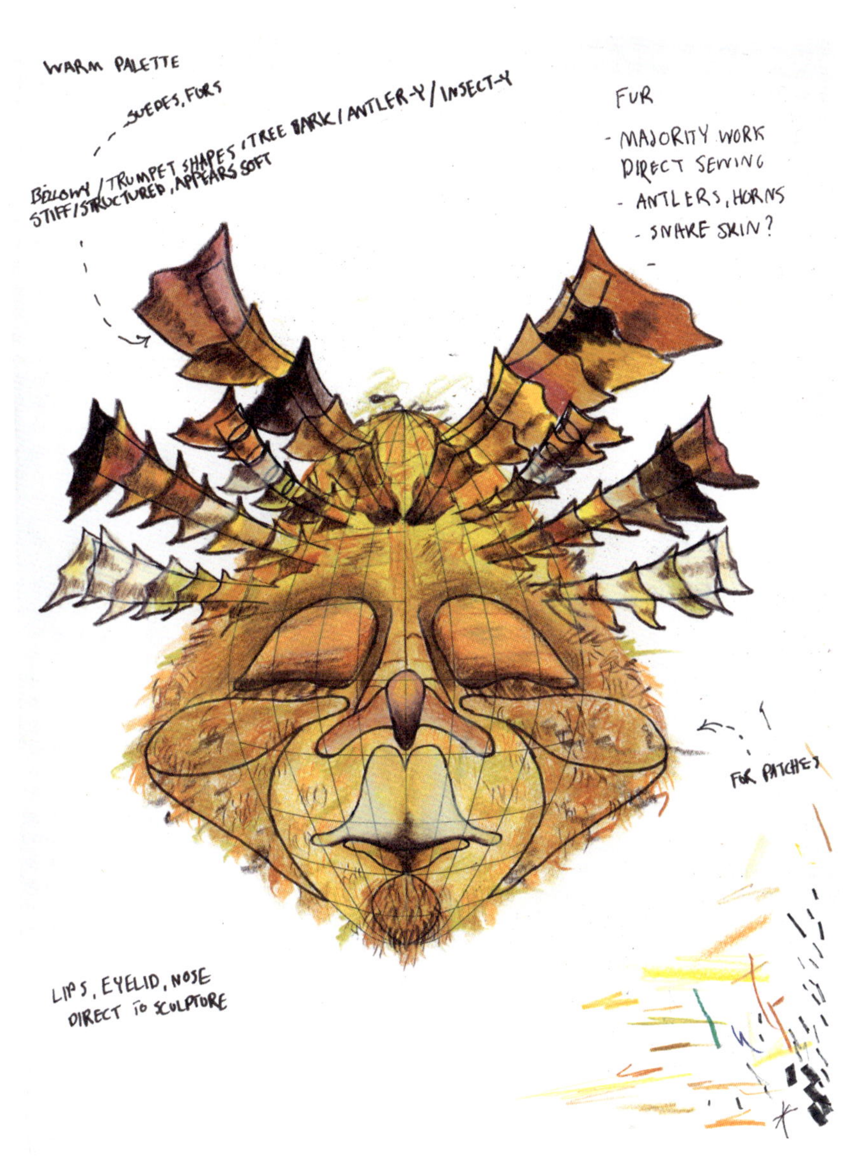
WARM PALETTE
- SUEDES, FURS
BELLOWY / TRUMPET SHAPES / TREE BARK / ANTLER-Y / INSECT-Y
STIFF / STRUCTURED, APPEARS SOFT
FUR
- MAJORITY WORK
  DIRECT SEWING
- ANTLERS, HORNS
- SNAKE SKIN?
-
FUR PATCHES
LIPS, EYELID, NOSE
DIRECT TO SCULPTURE

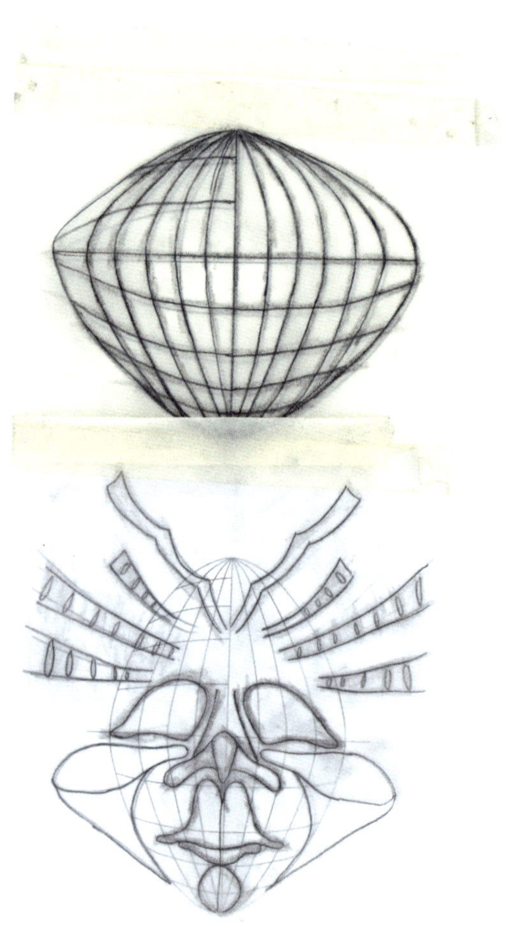

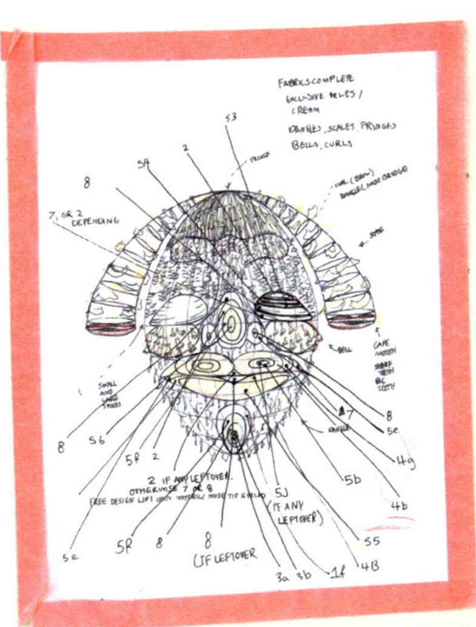

NOSE: USE 56 AS SIZE/SHAPE REFERANCE FOR REMAINING OUTER RINGS 56 NEEDS TO BE BACKED, BACK IT WITH 5J, EXTEND ITS EDJES SO 5J SHOWS, MAYBE BY 1.5 - 2 INCHES. SECOND RING (5f) SHOULD BE SLIMMER THAN IT APPEARS IN DRAWING, 3 IN DEPTH. THIRD RING (ANY COMBINATION OF GROUP 2) CAN BE MADE SLIMMER TO ACCOMMODATE (SAVE ENOUGH FOR) OTHER AREAS: NOSTRILS, EYE LIDS, CHIN.

EYELID: 54 WILL BE CUT INTO HALVES, SAME SIZE/SHAPE, EDJES CURVED, THIN END POINTED TOWARD NOSE, WIDE END TO EDJE OF FACE, BACKED WITH 5f, ABOUT AN INCH OF 5F AROUND. NEXT IS 53, WIDEST PART IN THE CENTER OF THE EYELID, BACK WITH 5E, ABOUT 1 - 1.5 IN DEPTH, ROUND EDJES OF 53.

MOUTH: 4b IS THE WIDEST RING, USE THE INTERESTING/SCUFFY PARTS, 5e, OUTERMOST RING, USE THE INTERESTING PARTS, ESPECIALLY WITH RED/PINK MARKINGS.

BOTTOM LIP (56) IS THE SWATH, EDJES WILL BE CUT + ROUNDED, PLOT SURROUNDING RINGS ACCORDINGLY, 5e and 4b LAYERS, USE INTERESTING PARTS.

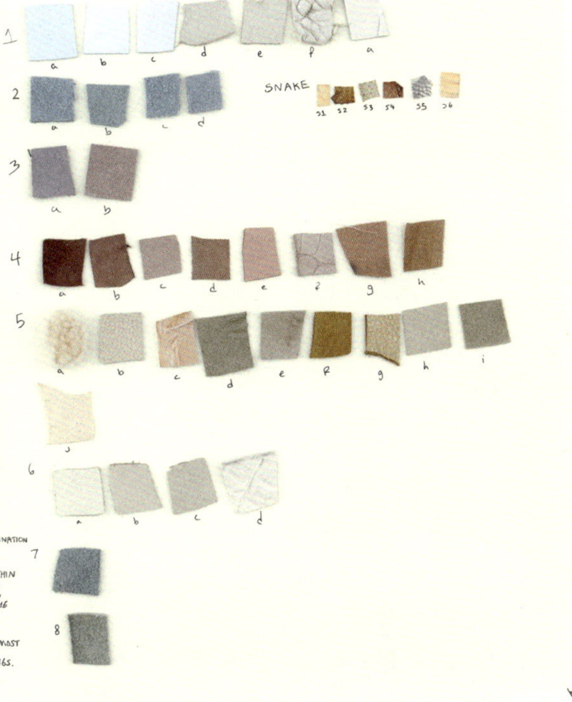

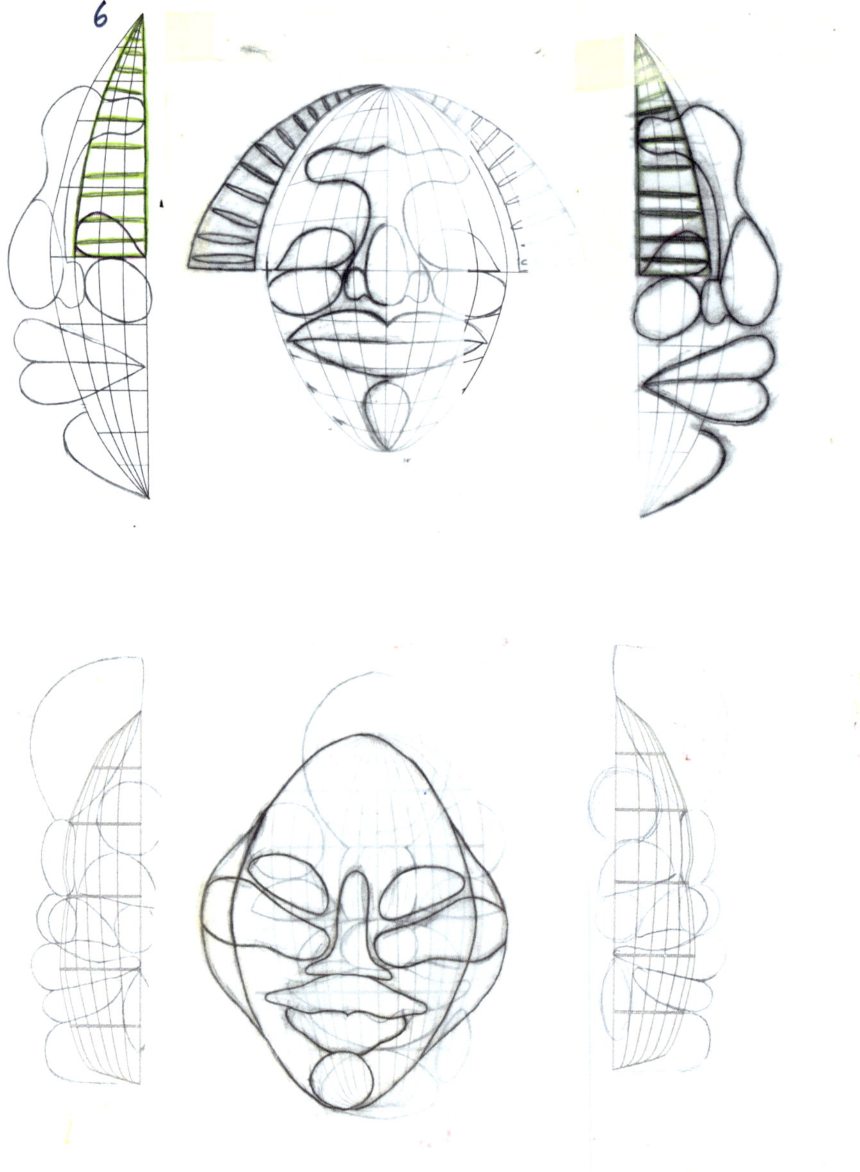

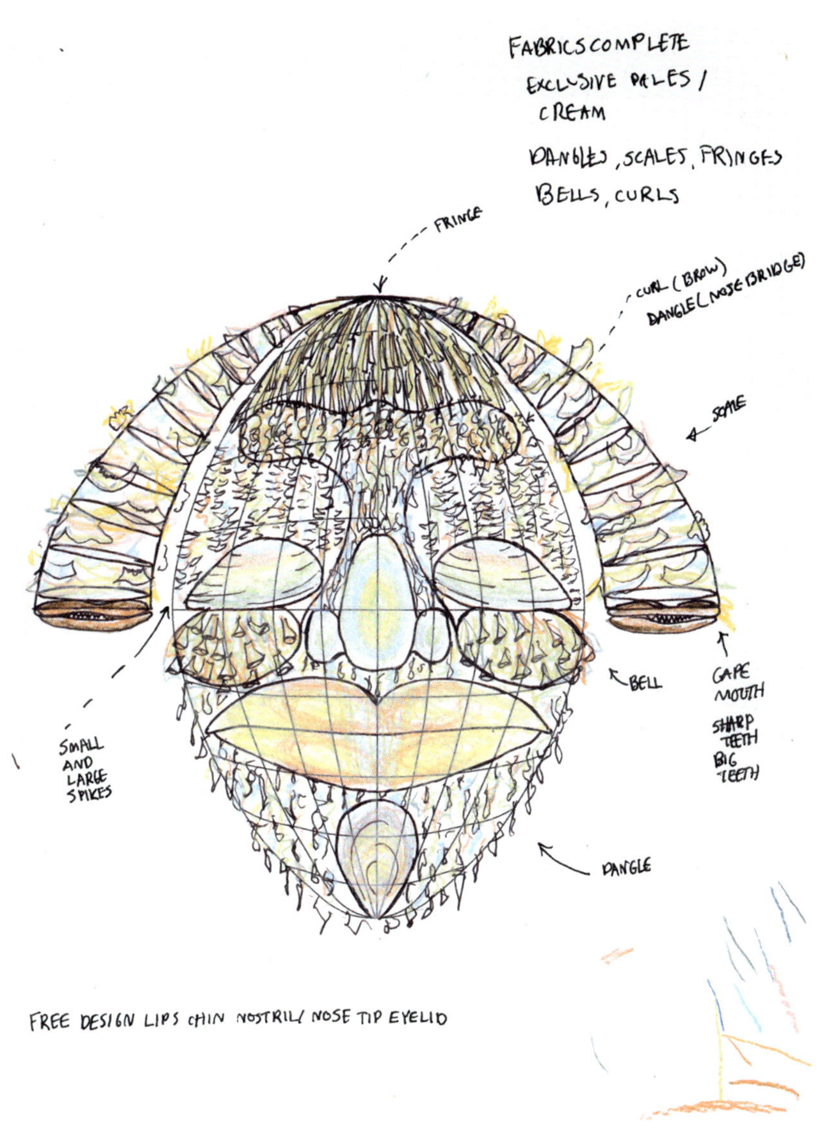
FABRICS COMPLETE
EXCLUSIVE PALES /
CREAM
DANGLES, SCALES, FRINGES
BELLS, CURLS
FRINGE
CURL (BROW)
DANGLE (NOSE BRIDGE)
SCALE
SMALL AND LARGE SPIKES
BELL
GAPE MOUTH
SHARP TEETH BIG TEETH
DANGLE
FREE DESIGN LIPS CHIN NOSTRIL NOSE TIP EYELID

COLOUR DESIGN PANEL — 'SUSURRUS' FLOWERS

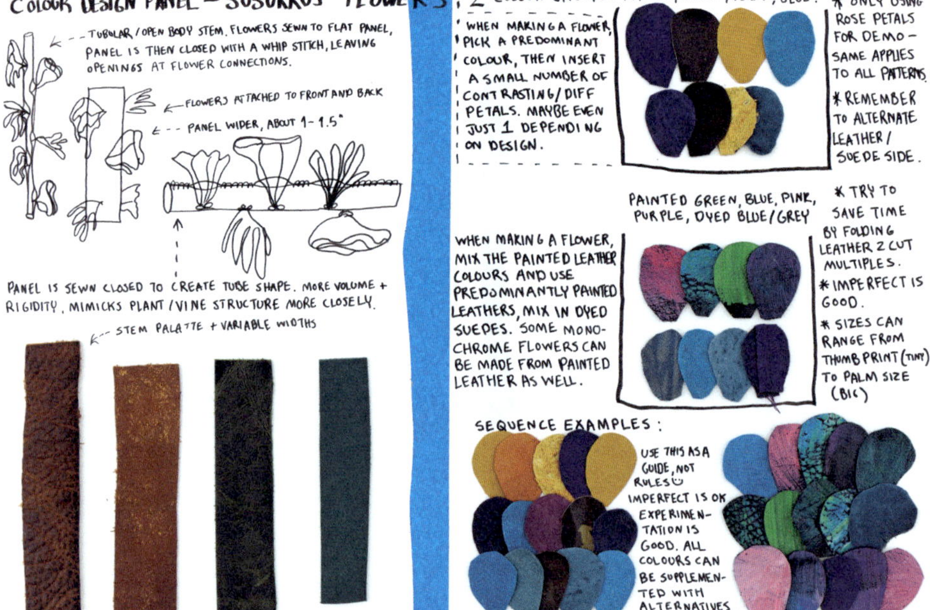

- TUBULAR / OPEN BODY STEM. FLOWERS SEWN TO FLAT PANEL. PANEL IS THEN CLOSED WITH A WHIP STITCH, LEAVING OPENINGS AT FLOWER CONNECTIONS.

← FLOWERS ATTACHED TO FRONT AND BACK

← PANEL WIDER, ABOUT 1 - 1.5"

PANEL IS SEWN CLOSED TO CREATE TUBE SHAPE. MORE VOLUME + RIGIDITY, MIMICKS PLANT / VINE STRUCTURE MORE CLOSELY.

← STEM PALATTE + VARIABLE WIDTHS

2 COLOUR GROUPS: PURPLE, BROWN, YELLOW, BLUE:

WHEN MAKING A FLOWER, PICK A PREDOMINANT COLOUR, THEN INSERT A SMALL NUMBER OF CONTRASTING / DIFF PETALS. MAYBE EVEN JUST 1 DEPENDING ON DESIGN.

* ONLY USING ROSE PETALS FOR DEMO — SAME APPLIES TO ALL PATTERNS.

* REMEMBER TO ALTERNATE LEATHER / SUEDE SIDE.

PAINTED GREEN, BLUE, PINK, PURPLE, DYED BLUE / GREY

WHEN MAKING A FLOWER, MIX THE PAINTED LEATHER COLOURS AND USE PREDOMINANTLY PAINTED LEATHERS, MIX IN DYED SUEDES. SOME MONO-CHROME FLOWERS CAN BE MADE FROM PAINTED LEATHER AS WELL.

* TRY TO SAVE TIME BY FOLDING LEATHER 2 CUT MULTIPLES.

* IMPERFECT IS GOOD.

* SIZES CAN RANGE FROM THUMB PRINT (TINY) TO PALM SIZE (BIG)

SEQUENCE EXAMPLES:

USE THIS AS A GUIDE, NOT RULES ☺ IMPERFECT IS OK EXPERIMEN-TATION IS GOOD. ALL COLOURS CAN BE SUPPLEMEN-TED WITH ALTERNATIVES.

COLOUR DESIGN
GREEN BLUE BROWN - MODERATE
YELLOW / MUSTARD (MODERATE)
PURPLE (MODERATE)

- MAJORITY WORK
  DIRECT SEWING
- GATHERED LAYERS
- FLOWER VINES
-

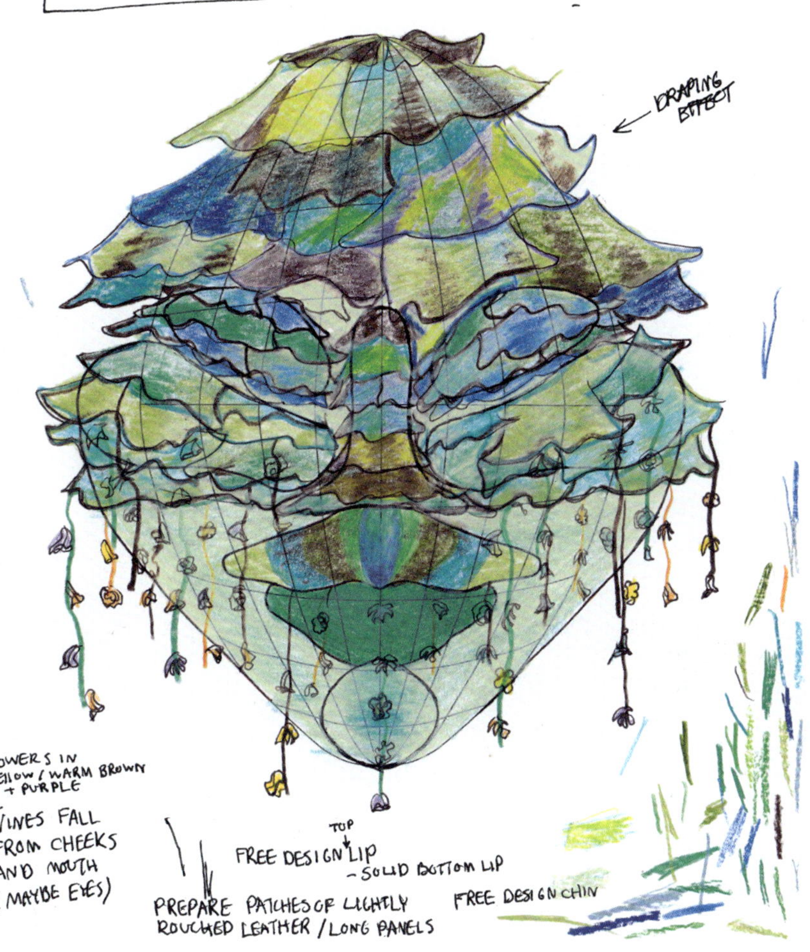

FLOWERS IN
YELLOW / WARM BROWN
+ PURPLE

VINES FALL
FROM CHEEKS
AND MOUTH
(MAYBE EYES)

TOP
FREE DESIGN LIP
- SOLID BOTTOM LIP

PREPARE PATCHES OF LIGHTLY
ROUCHED LEATHER / LONG PANELS

FREE DESIGN CHIN

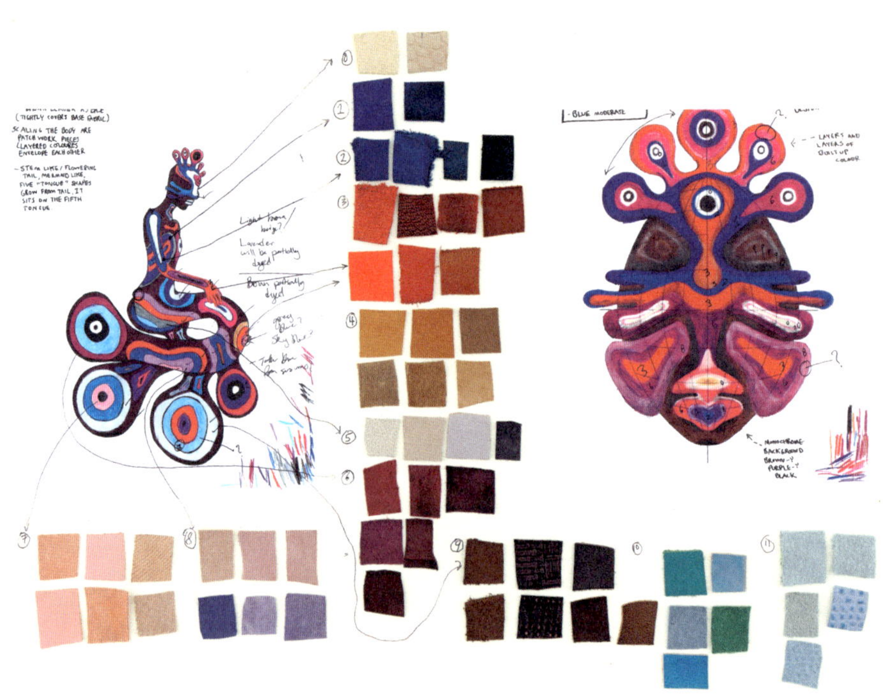

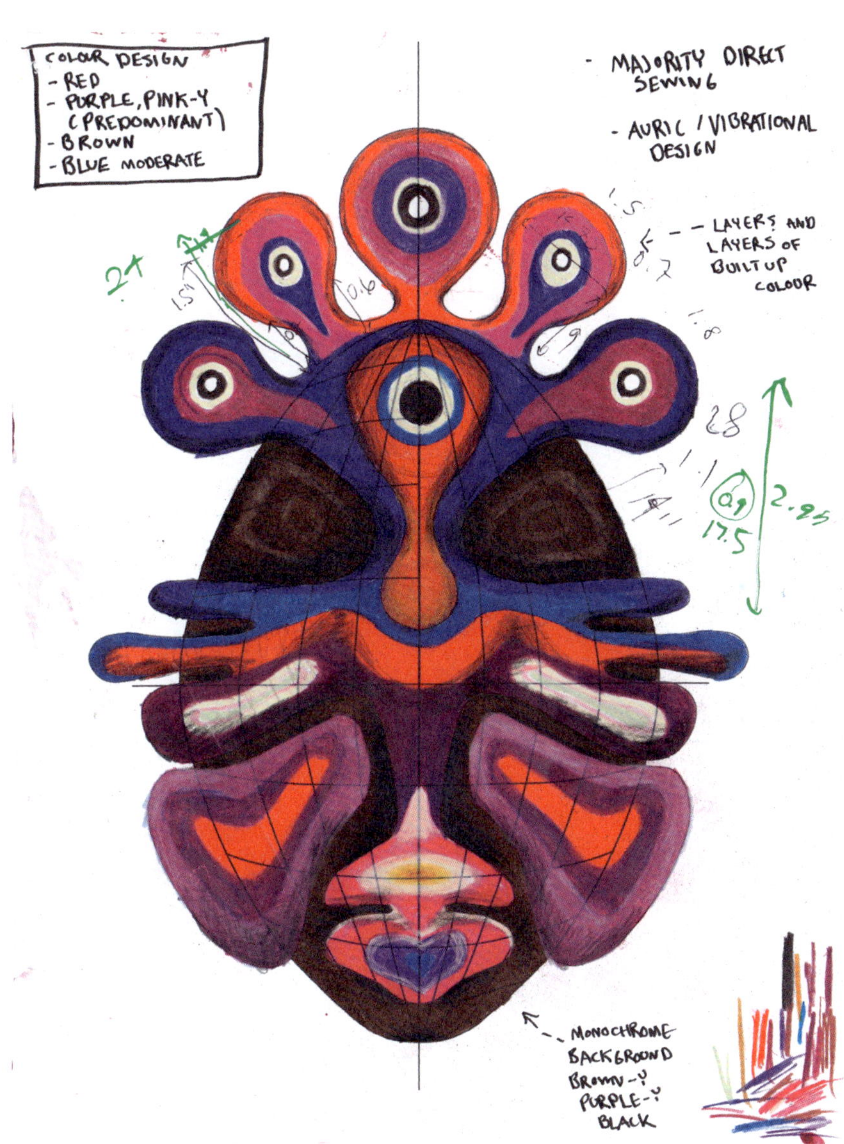
COLOUR DESIGN
- RED
- PURPLE, PINK-Y
  (PREDOMINANT)
- BROWN
- BLUE MODERATE
- MAJORITY DIRECT
  SEWING
- AURIC / VIBRATIONAL
  DESIGN
- - LAYERS AND
  LAYERS OF
  BUILT UP
  COLOUR
MONOCHROME
BACKGROUND
BROWN-Y
PURPLE-Y
BLACK

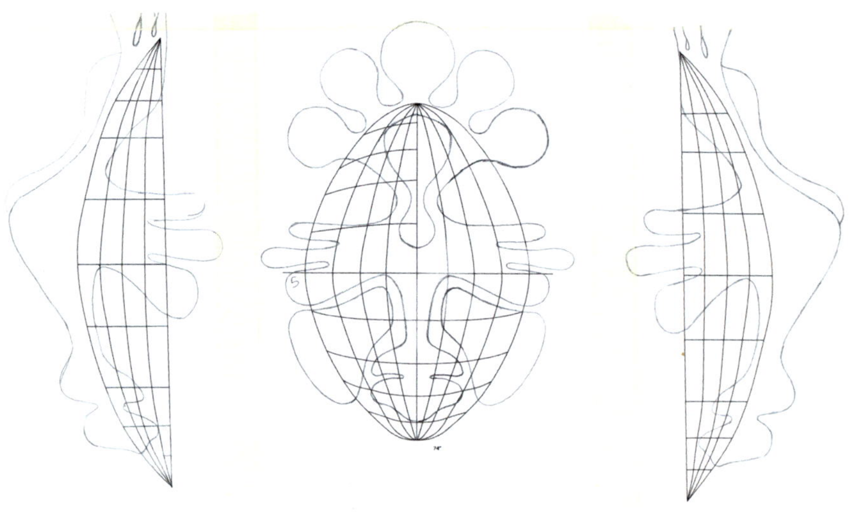

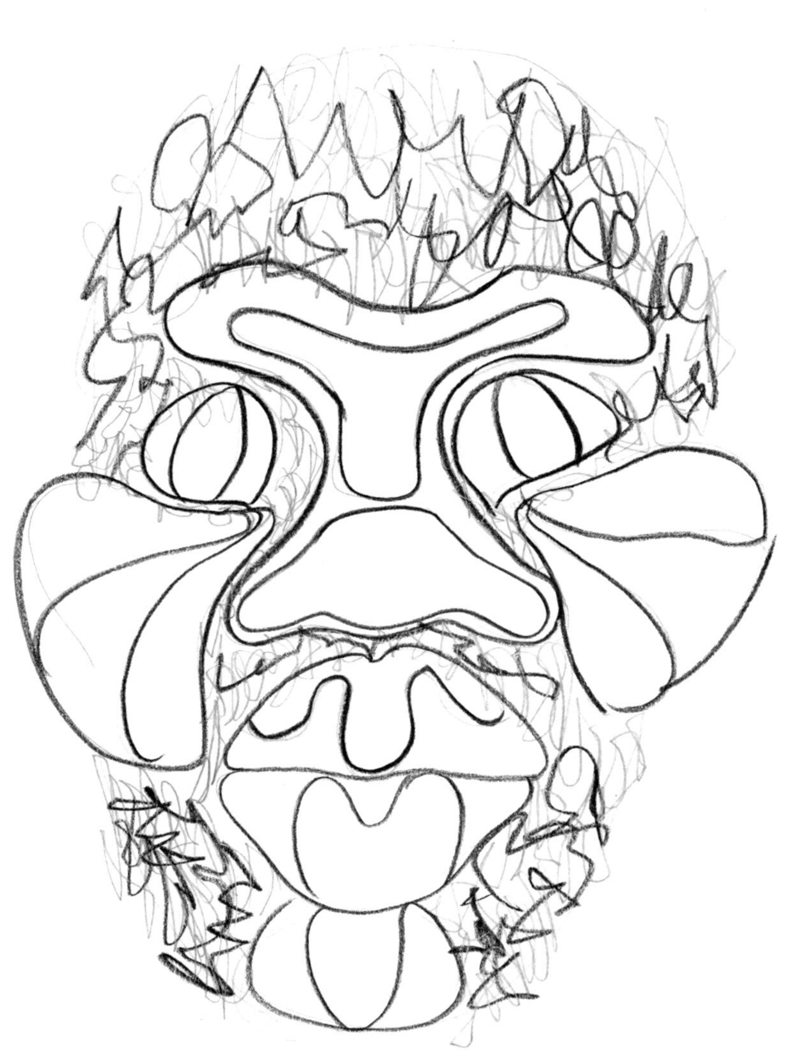

NUMBERS 3 and 4 ARE OUT OF ORDER ON THE DIAGRAM, SORRY

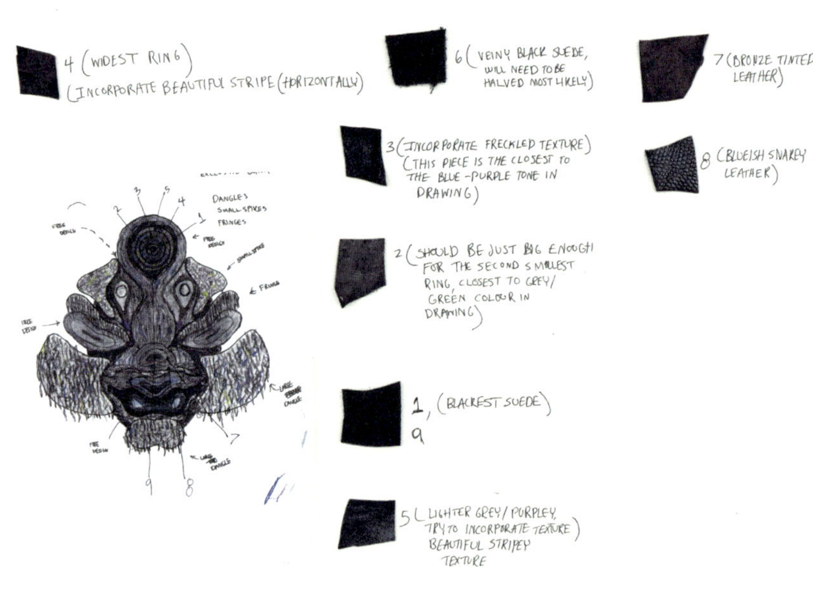

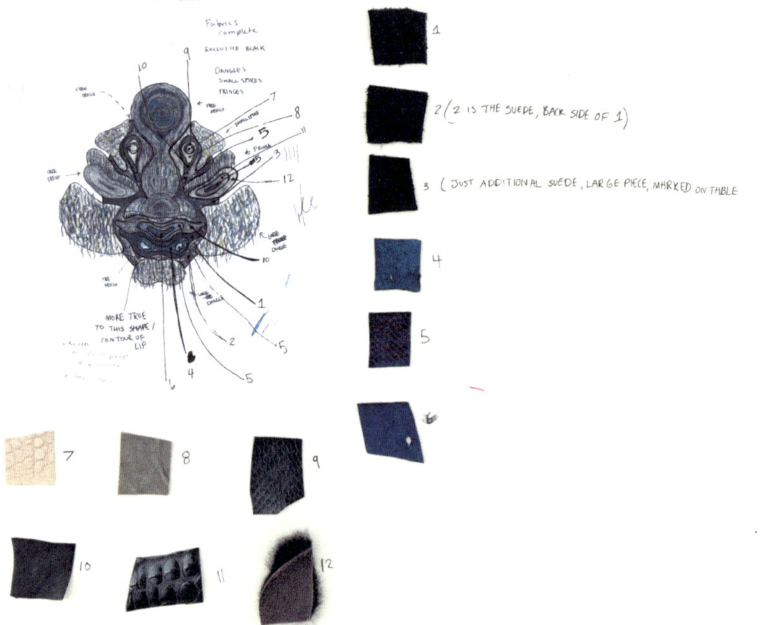

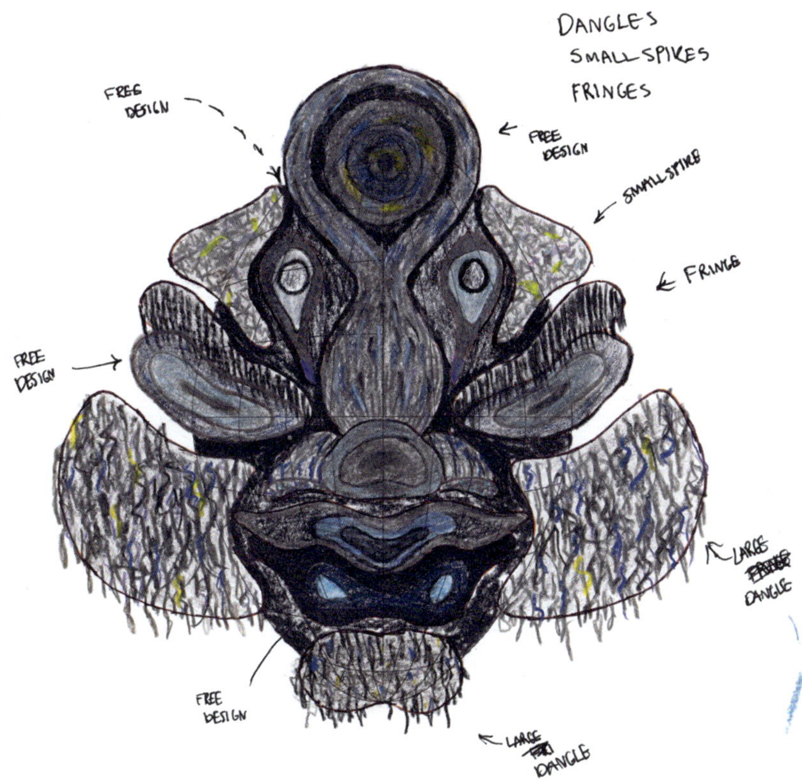

TRIDENT
TRIDENTIS
Fabrics complete
EXCLUSIVE BLACK
DANGLES
SMALL SPIKES
FRINGES
FREE DESIGN
FREE DESIGN
SMALL SPIKE
FRINGE
FREE DESIGN
LARGE DANGLE
FREE DESIGN
LARGE DANGLE

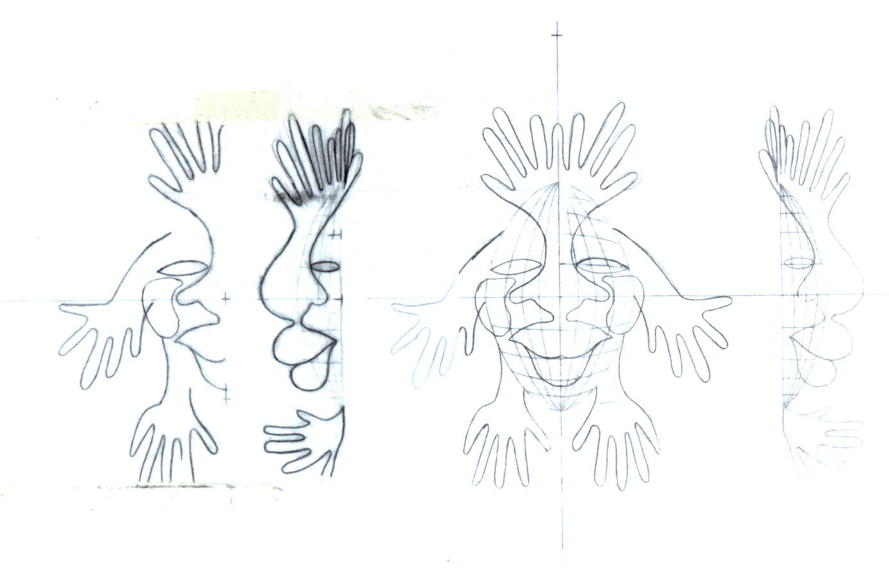

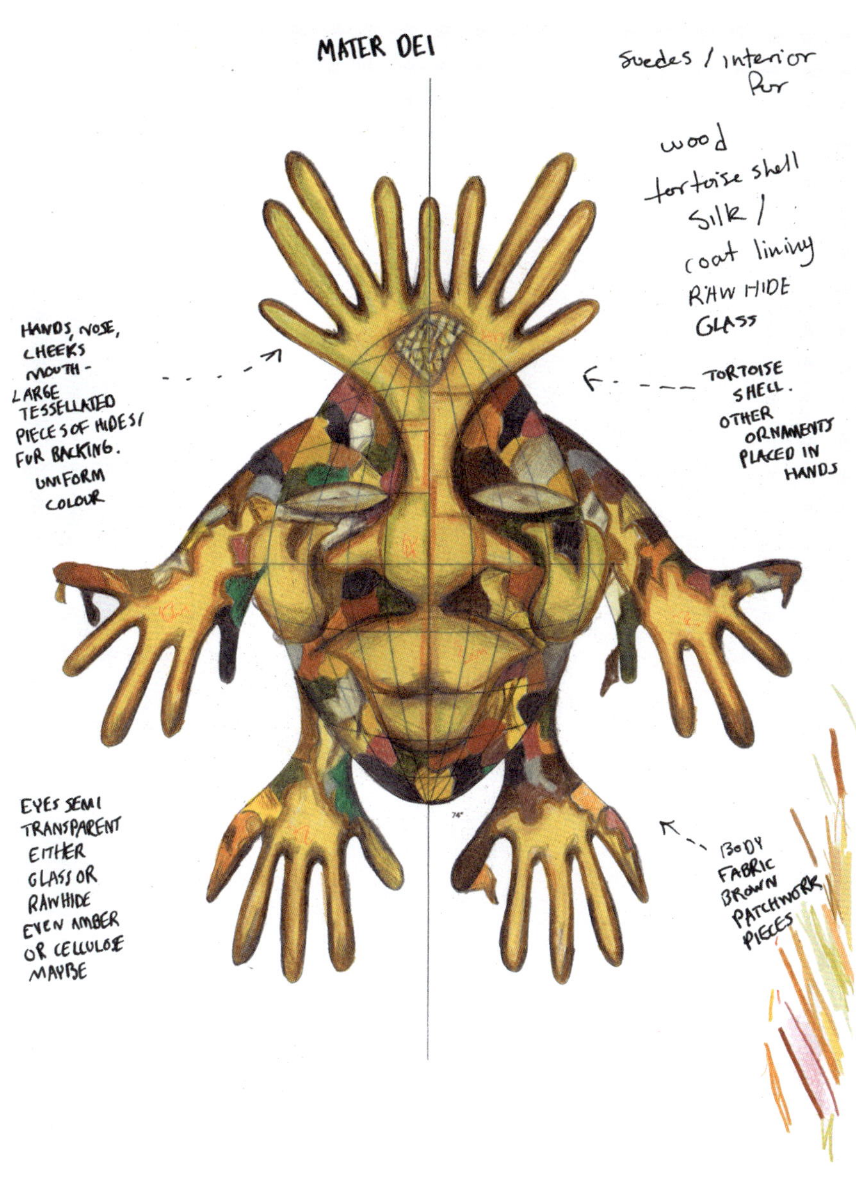
MATER DEI
Suedes / interior Fur
wood
tortoise shell
silk /
coat lining
RAW HIDE
GLASS
TORTOISE SHELL. OTHER ORNAMENTS PLACED IN HANDS
HANDS, NOSE, CHEEKS MOUTH - LARGE TESSELLATED PIECES OF HIDES/ FUR BACKING. UNIFORM COLOUR
EYES SEMI TRANSPARENT EITHER GLASS OR RAWHIDE EVEN AMBER OR CELLULOSE MAYBE
BODY FABRIC BROWN PATCHWORK PIECES

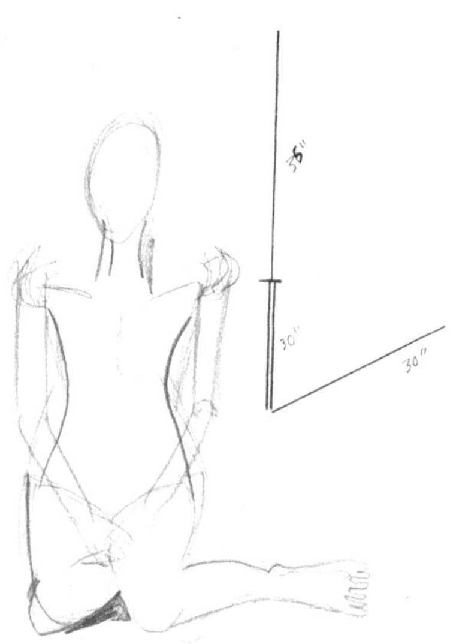
36"
30"
30"

~ BROWN LEATHER AS BASE
(TIGHTLY COVERS BASE FABRIC)

~ SCALING THE BODY ARE
PATCH WORK PIECES
LLAYERED COLOURES
ENVELOPE EACH OTHER

~ STEM LIKE / FLOWERING
TAIL, MERMAID LIKE,
FIVE "TONGUE" SHAPES
GROW FROM TAIL, IT
SITS ON THE FIFTH
TONGUE.

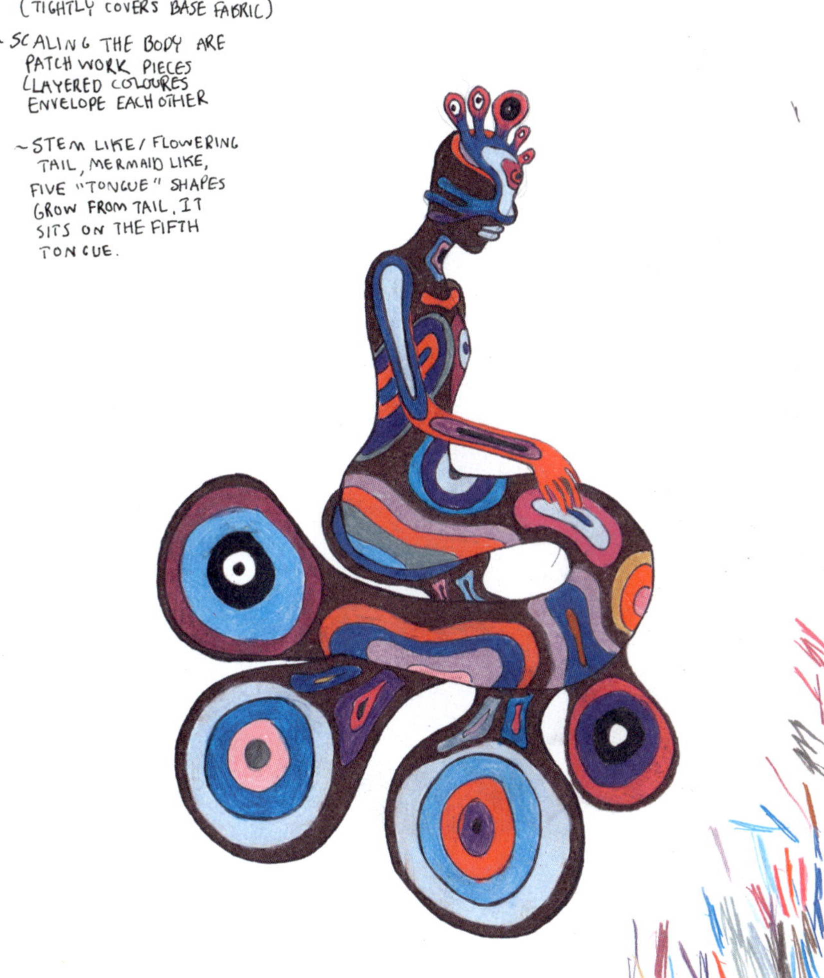

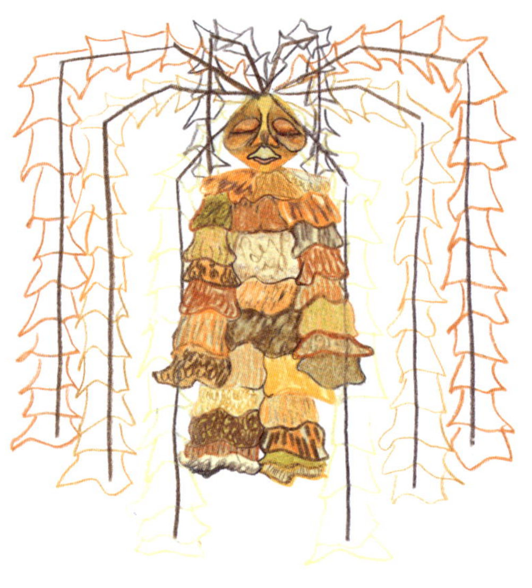

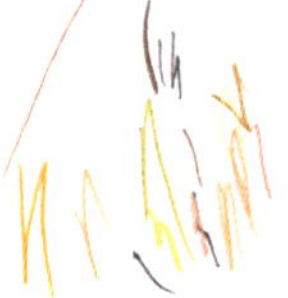

~ MUCH SMALLER PANELS COVER
HEAD/ FACE

~ SLIGHTLY SMALLER PANELS COVER
BODY

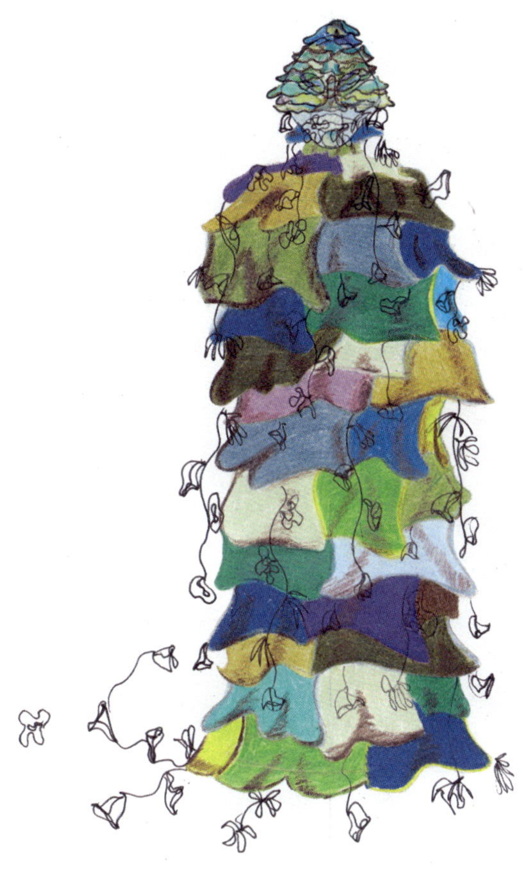
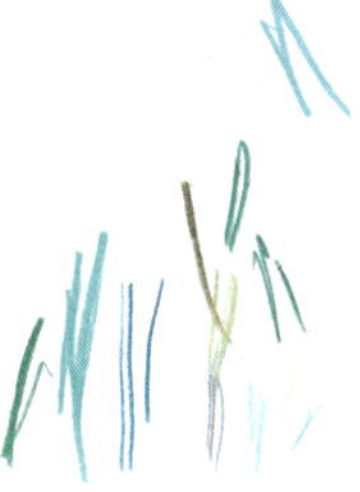

OUTER CLOAK MADE OF DANGLES

HANDS FEET SCULPTED IN RED LEATHER
HEAD/FACE SCULPTED IN LEATHERS + SUEDES + PAINTED LEATHER
CREATE ILLUSION OF BODY UNDER CLOAK
CREATE ILLUSION OF RED INTERIOR AROUND HEAD
UNDER CLOAK

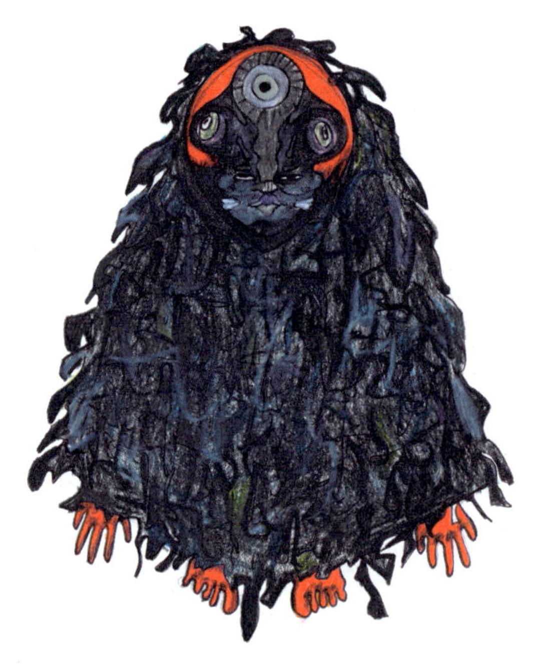

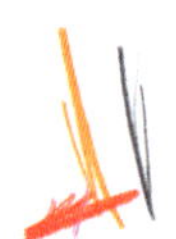

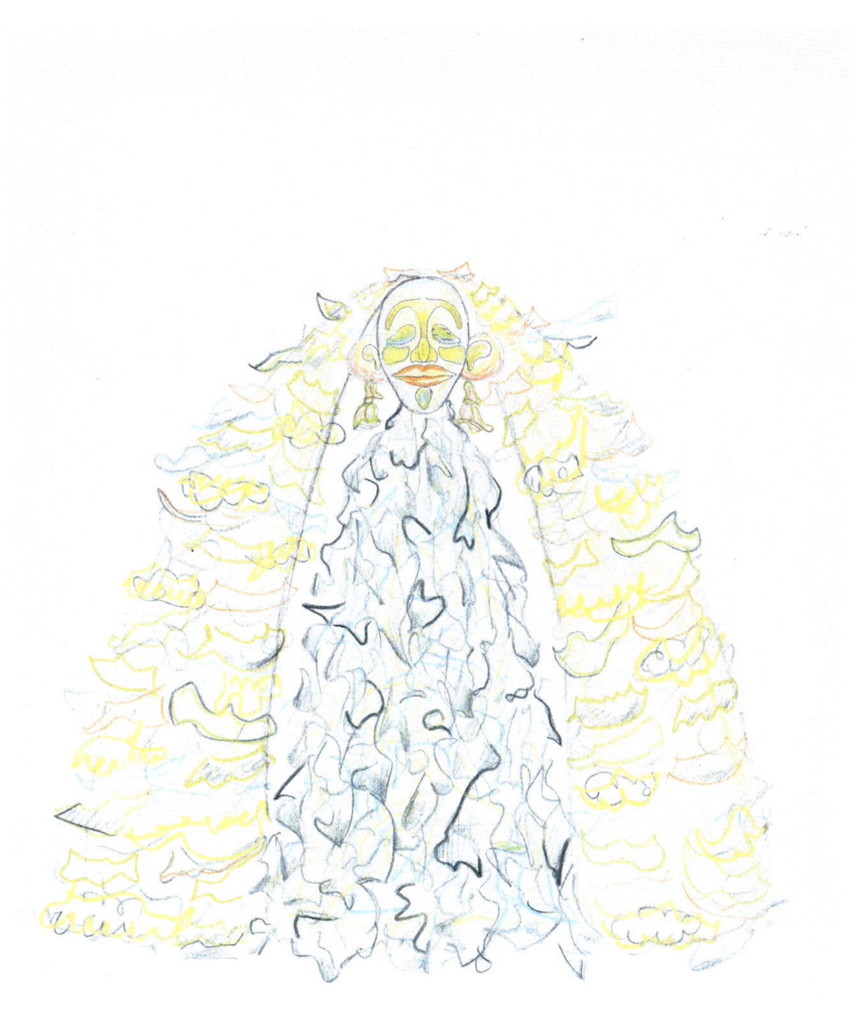

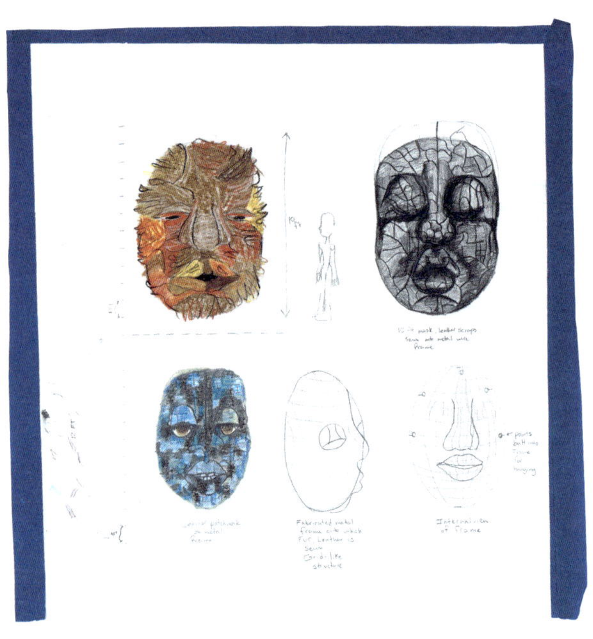
15 ft mask, leather scraps
sewn onto metal wire
frame

Leather patchwork
on metal
frame

Fabricated metal
frame onto which
fur leather is
sewn
Grid-like
structure

points
butt into
frame
for
hanging

Internal view
of frame

~ FACE SCULPTED IN
LEATHER
~ BASE FABRIC ADORNED
WITH MIXED HIDES/
FUR BACK
~ FEET SCULPTED IN LEATHER
~ ARMS SCULPTED IN LEATHER
~ LEGS/PANT IS BROWN
PATCHWORK PIECES
"WINGS" "HAIR"
CHEST + TORSO
MIXED HIDES

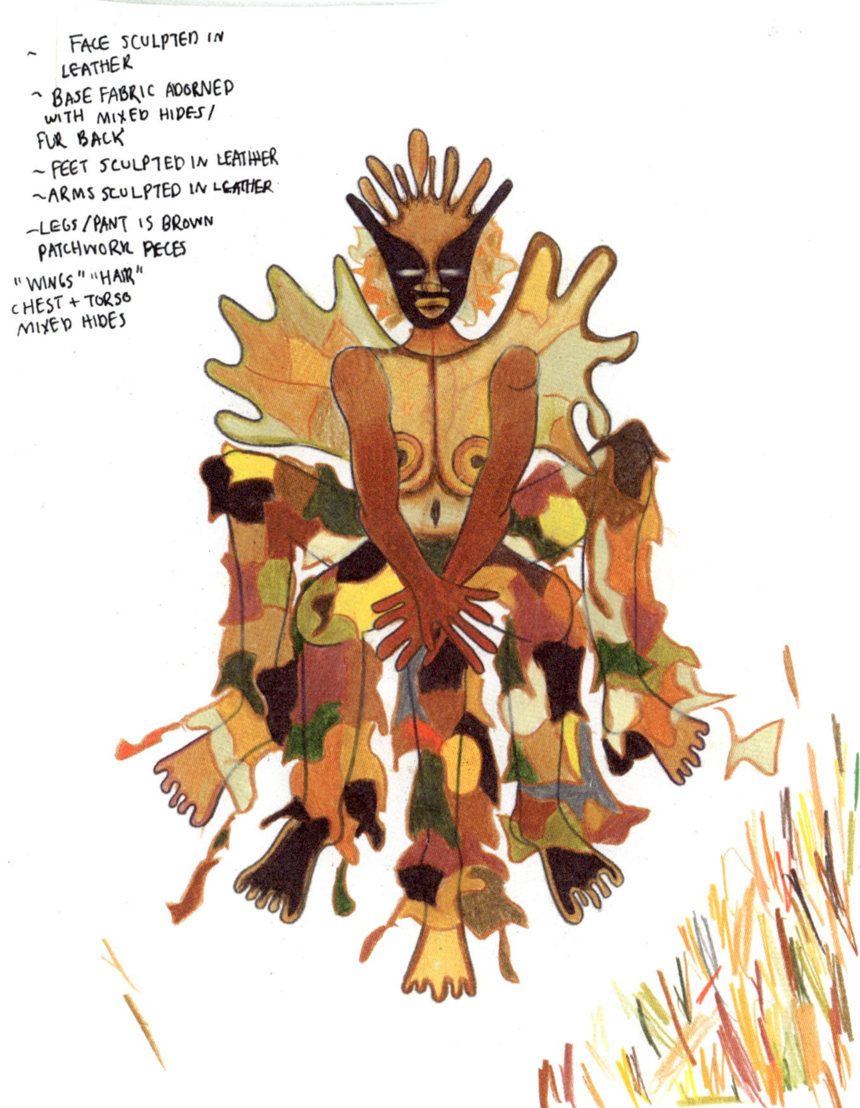

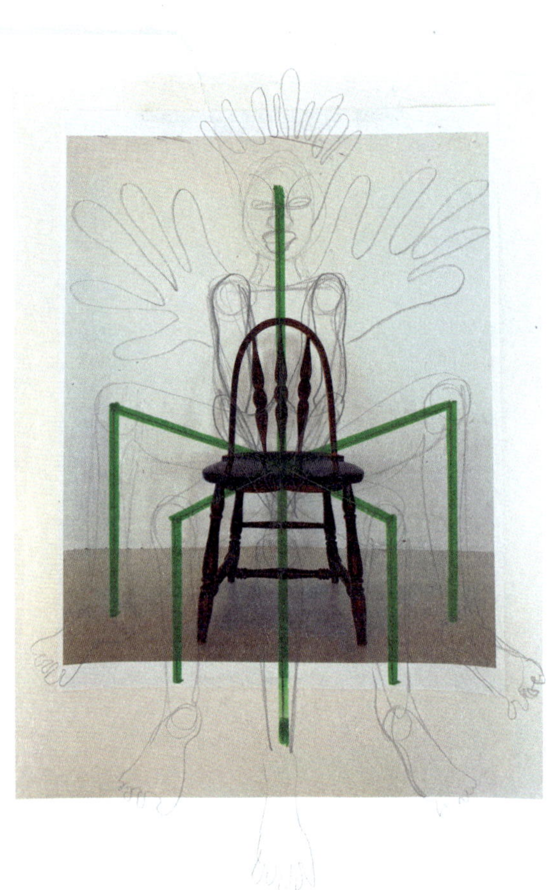

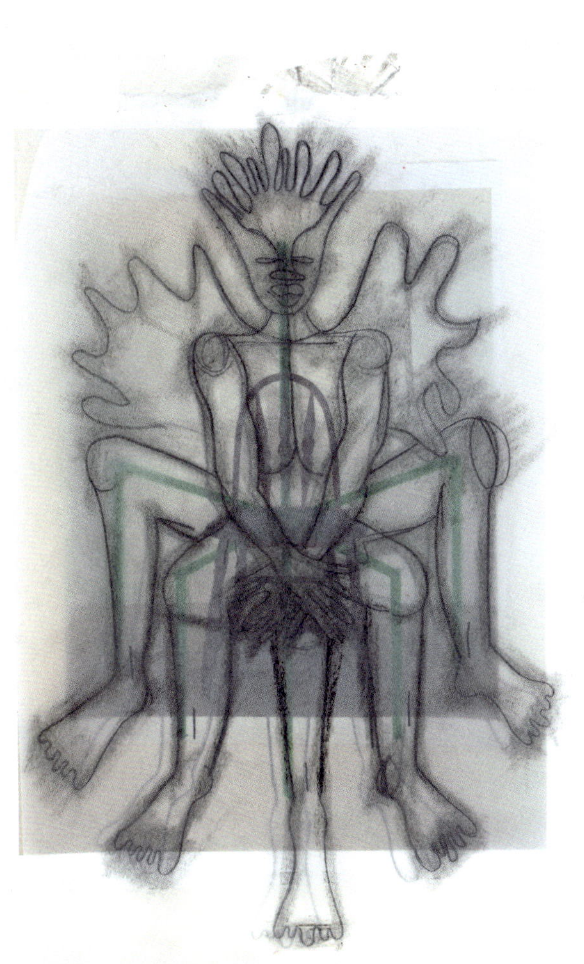

Study, 2016
Repurposed leather, fur, suede, organic cotton twill, and coated nylon thread
11 ½ × 8 × 3 ¾ inches | 29.2 × 20.3 × 9.5 cm

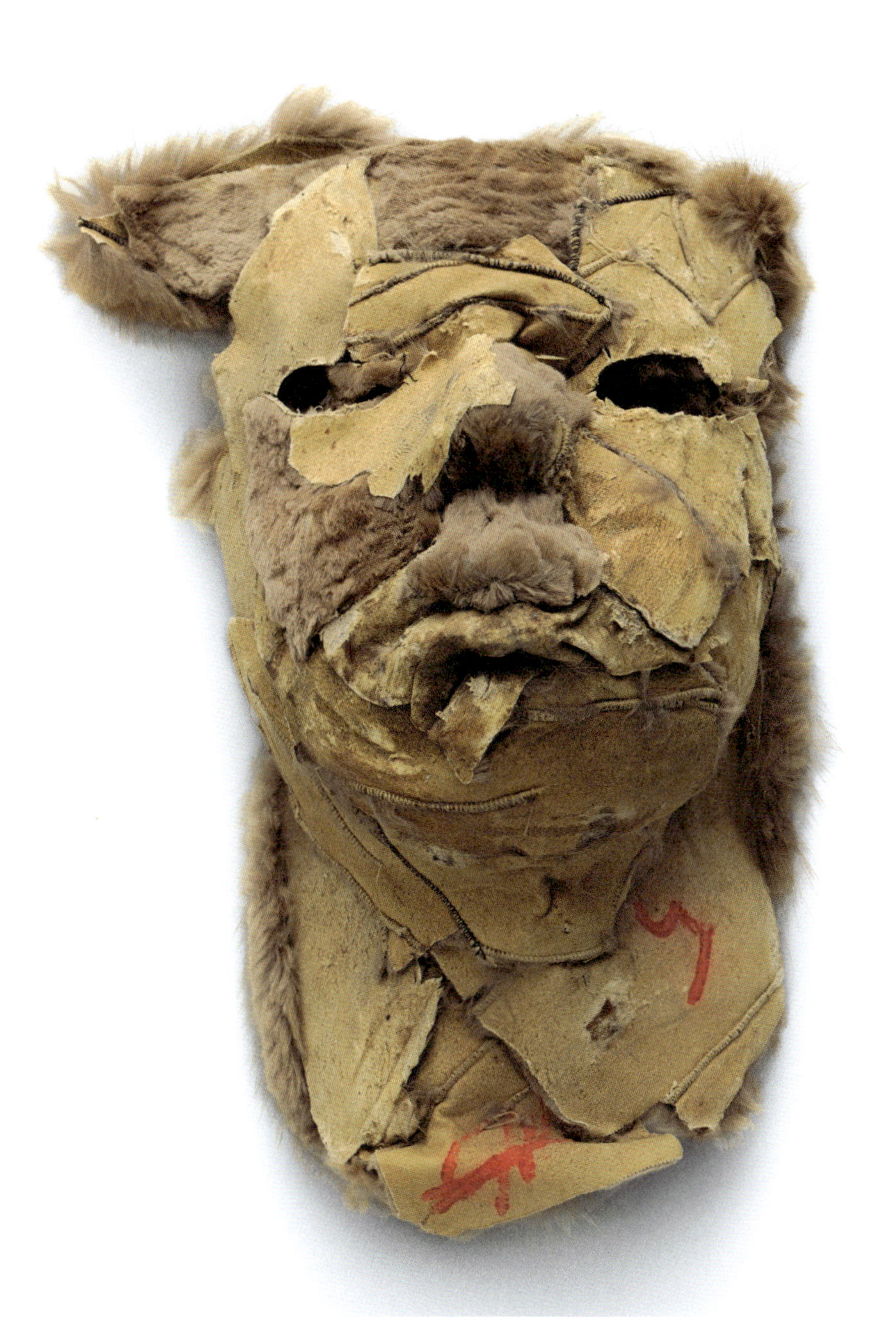

David Zwirner and Ebony L. Haynes wish to thank Tau Lewis, without whom this exhibition and publication would not have been possible. Thanks are due to Tiana Reid for her illuminating text and to Yves B. Golden for contributing a poem to this volume.

For their work on the exhibition, we are grateful to Rebecca Ashby-Colón, Claire Ball, Susan Cernek, Allison Chipak, Cristina Covucci, Karryl Eugene, Maris Hutchinson, Felice Jiang, Coco Kim, Vida Lercari, Julia Lukacher, Kerry McFate, Clive Murphy, Julian Phillips, Robert Richburg, Gabriela Scopazzi, Virginia Stroh, and Nora Woodin.

Thank you to Andrea Hyde for the catalogue series design and, for their work on this volume, to Sergio Brunelli, Luke Chase, Anna Drozda, Fabio Ferrandini, Zeno Ferrandini, Doro Globus, Elizabeth Gordon, Jessica Palinski Hoos, Amy Hordes, Daniela Ioan, Jordan Kelly, Mari Perina, Molly Stein, Jules Thomson, Joey Young, and Lucas Zwirner.

The artist would like to thank Patty Kelly for her unwavering support of her career; David Zwirner and Ebony L. Haynes for their support and hard work in making the exhibition and publication happen; and Zach Caruso, Jeorge Galutia, Zoe Hochman, Avia Hurley, Isabel Powis, Bobby Smith, and Loretta Violante, without whom the show would not have come to be.

Collections

p. 8 (bottom): Kimbell Art Museum, Fort Worth, Texas
p. 25: Collection of Aubrey Graham
p. 29: Collection of the Rubio Butterfield Foundation
p. 39: Private collection
p. 43: San Francisco Museum of Modern Art. Accessions Committee Fund purchase, by exchange, through a gift of Michael D. Abrams, 2023
p. 47: Collection of Jay Smith and Laura Rapp
p. 51: Rennie Collection, Vancouver
p. 55: Collection of Bertil Schuil
p. 59: Private collection
p. 63: Private collection
p. 67: Miller Meigs Collection
pp. 71, 72, 73, 74 (top and bottom), 75, 76, 77, 78, 79, 80, 81, 82 (top and bottom), 83, 84, 85, 86, 87, 88, 89, 90, 91, 92, 93, 94, 95, 97: Collection of the artist

Photography

p. 8 (top): Courtesy Billy Rose Theatre Division, The New York Public Library for the Performing Arts
p. 13: Photo by Laura Findlay, courtesy Oakville Galleries
pp. 20–21, 22–23, 36–37, 55, 57, 63, 65, 67, 68–69, 71, 72, 73, 74 (top and bottom), 75, 76, 77, 78, 79, 80, 81, 82 (top and bottom), 83, 84, 85, 86, 87, 88, 89, 90, 91, 92, 93, 94, 95, 97: Maris Hutchinson
pp. 25, 26–27, 29, 30–31, 33, 35, 39, 41, 43, 45, 47, 49, 51, 53, 59, 61: Kerry McFate

The *Clarion* series is an essential component of 52 Walker programming. An edition accompanies every exhibition, highlighting and expanding on the show's conceptual theses through newly commissioned texts, interviews, archival materials, and artistic interventions. The series is named in honor of the renowned author Octavia E. Butler, who was first published in the 1971 Clarion Science Fiction and Fantasy Writers' Workshop anthology.

Other Titles in the *Clarion* Series
I. Kandis Williams: A Line
II. Nikita Gale: END OF SUBJECT
III. Nora Turato: govern me harder
IV. Tiona Nekkia McClodden: MASK / CONCEAL / CARRY

Forthcoming Titles
VI. Gordon Matta-Clark and Pope.L: Impossible Failures
VII. Bob Thompson: So let us all be citizens

Published by 52 Walker and
David Zwirner Books
on the occasion of

Tau Lewis: Vox Populi, Vox Dei
52 Walker, New York
October 28, 2022–January 7, 2023

52 Walker
52 Walker Street
New York, New York 10013
+1 212 727 1961
52walker.com

David Zwirner Books
520 West 20th Street, 2nd Floor
New York, New York 10011
+1 212 727 2070
davidzwirnerbooks.com

Editor: Ebony L. Haynes
Project Editor: Elizabeth Gordon
Editorial Coordinator: Jessica Palinski Hoos
Proofreader: Anna Drozda

Design: Andrea Hyde
Photography coordination: Rebecca Ashby-Colón,
 Virginia Stroh
Production: Luke Chase
Color separations: VeronaLibri, Verona
Printing: VeronaLibri, Verona

Typefaces: DTL Fleischmann, Genath
Paper: Magno Natural, 140 gsm

Publication
© 2023 52 Walker and David Zwirner Books

"Curator's Note: The Ghost"
 © 2023 Ebony L. Haynes

"What the People Are Like: Voices from Without"
 © 2023 Tiana Reid

"Spring to the 1st Magnitude"
 © 2023 Yves B. Golden

All artwork by Tau Lewis
 © 2023 Tau Lewis

ISBN 978-1-64423-114-2

Library of Congress Control Number: 2023938452

Printed in Italy

Notes

Notes

Notes